WALSALL'S ENGINE SHED

RAILWAYMEN'S MEMORIES 1877–1968

45680

WALSALL'S ENGINE SHED

RAILWAYMEN'S MEMORIES 1877–1968

3C

JACK HADDOCK

The History Press

Frontispiece: 45680 on turntable after working into Walsall on the Pines Express, 1960.

This book is dedicated to the late Joyce Hammond of Pelsall, local historian, who was for many years Senior Archives/Local Studies Assistant at Walsall Local History Centre.

Joyce was instrumental in organising, listing and making available the Jack Haddock Collection of photographs and oral history recordings at that centre, and without her hard work, which continued after her retirement, this book would have been much more difficult to write and illustrate.

Joyce passed away in April 2006, and is well remembered as a good friend and a fine colleague by all who knew and worked with her.

First published by Tempus Publishing in 2006

Reprinted in 2016 by

The History Press
The Mill, Brimscombe Port
Stroud, Gloucestershire, GL5 2QG
www.thehistorypress.co.uk

British Library Cataloguing in Publication Data.
A catalogue record for this book is available from the British Library.

ISBN 978 0 7524 4034 7

Typesetting and origination by Tempus Publishing Limited

Contents

Acknowledgements

Special thanks go to Jack Boulton (driver at Ryecroft and locomotive inspector at Saltley), Fred Haywood (driver at Ryecroft) and Frank Rigby (fitter at Ryecroft and shedmaster at Bushbury), for their proof-reading of the original manuscripts.

I would like to thank the staff of the Walsall Local History Centre, past and present, for the use of the Centre's Archive Department for the storage of my documents, writings, slides and tapes concerning my research into Walsall's railway history. This includes much oral history of the many railway staff (management, maintenance, footplate and artisan) from Midland, L&NWR and British Rail periods, and especially of Ryecroft shed. Many of those quoted in these pages were not only my near neighbours, they were also friends. The deposition of this mass of material in the Centre will ensure its survival for posterity and availability for possible future research, and insight into the workings of 3C Ryecroft.

My thanks are due to Stuart Williams for reproducing many images from my negative collection for this and other articles I have written. These cover railway, bus and canal subjects, especially from my No.162 railway archive section. I want to thank Mrs Pat Everiss for her considerable help and for her patience, time and skill in typing my original manuscripts; also Robert Selvey, for his help in typing some of my later penned notes into a suitable presentation for publication, scanning photographs, typing and proof-reading the final draft before finally sending it for publication. I also extend my thanks to Bob Essery for the time spent scanning my flat documents into electronic form.

Thanks must also go to David Spires for encouragement, correspondence and assistance; to John Bucknall for his help in editing the mass of material into something approaching a book; and to Ken Mottram for a second proof-reading once John's work was complete.

Lastly, a note of thanks to the photographers, past and present, who have made their work available for use in this publication. Their time, skill and willing co-operation have been much appreciated.

As you can see, a work of this nature relies on the help and support of more people than those credited with the work. My sincere thanks go to each and every one of those named here. Their help will ensure that 3C Ryecroft lives on!

Introduction

This book is not a meticulous clinical history of Walsall's railway system. If classification is needed, it can be looked upon as a record of local railway life, as told by men from the now-closed Ryecroft shed. It mentions the vibrant, intense activity of Walsall Station and its Long Street and Midland goods yards, which during the period 1879 to 1957 were the focal point of travel and commerce in the West Midland town. Walsall became a Borough, then a Metropolitan Borough, reflecting its growth and importance.

My interest in Walsall's railway system and infrastructure was brought about by virtue of living within five minutes' walk from Ryecroft shed and having relatives who worked on the station, living in Long Street overlooking the ex-L&NWR and Midland Railway goods yard. Such was the importance of the railway to the town that, as the traffic in the area developed, Bescot locomotive shed and its vast marshalling yard was built in 1892 on the outskirts of Walsall, to aid freight distribution throughout the nearby Black Country industrial conurbation; and to deliver its production by rail to far-away destinations and markets. Living from 1929 within hearing and smelling distance of the Webb-designed Northlight engine shed, until its closure to steam traction in 1957, I became obsessed with local railway life and lore. Over the years I associated with many hundreds of railwaymen who resided in the North Walsall and Butts districts near the shed. It has been a privilege to know most of this fine body of working men who, individually, gave up to fifty years of service to the public and the commerce of the town of Walsall. Their remarkable record speaks for itself; no serious accident has taken place on the railways in Walsall involving loss of life. Sadly, there have been fatalities, but from the turn of the century to the present day, Walsall's railwaymen have an excellent safety record in daily operation and dedication to duty.

Living so near to Ryecroft shed, as a youngster I was attracted to the sight and sounds of steam engines. A special memory of the 1930s was the shed's welcome to each New Year. My parents always allowed me to join other railway families to go to Ryecroft, or, if the weather was inclement, to listen from an open bedroom window, as shed staff saw in the New Year in fine style. Every engine in steam whistled and hooted its own welcome

A 1937 view of Ryecroft's coal plant with veteran ex-Midland loco 20157, which at this time was used mainly for permanent way engineer's inspection specials. There is a new Stanier tank on the right. (Stanley Webb)

Sunday view of Ryecroft shed with 'Super D' 49020, 1955. (Jack Haddock Collection)

to the New Year – a symphony of steam voices in solo and unison lasting for the first five minutes of 1 January. Sometimes, if the wind was from a southerly direction, Bescot's similar greeting could be heard if their celebration started a few seconds earlier. It was a very pleasant occasion looked forward to by the local railwaymen of that period who did their best to enjoy life despite the difficult conditions and most irregular hours which were the railwayman's lot.

Lying in bed on a calm summer's night, windows open for the blessing of a cooling breeze, I could hear the constant muffled sounds of shovels and fire irons at work as men toiled through the long night to prepare locomotives for early duty. These sounds were backed by the deeper, less staccato, rumblings from the mechanical coaling plant. After the last passenger locomotives came in for service and overnight rest, a constant procession of mineral and freight trains temporarily disturbed the night air. Sleep was often broken by the engines' exhaust as they worked their heavy trains – full regulator and cut off – up steep gradients to Cannock and Sutton, sometimes with bankers pushing at the rear of the train. All Ryecroft citizens were used to the uphill thrash throughout the night, and to many children who were train spotters, these sounds were their bedtime lullaby. My mother was born and bred in Long Street, and I made many visits to my grandmother's house, with its unique panoramic view of the goods yard. I spent many hours in the front bedroom of No.47, taking in the constant activity of men loading and unloading the various horse-drawn drays, and the larger and more substantial railway vans and wagons. In the foreground, an L&NWR coal engine's syncopated 'chaff-chaff' exhaust seemed to express determination as the locomotive shunted almost twenty-four hours a day. Over the main 'up and down' lines, a less abrasive Midland tank engine performed a similar duty near Tasker Street and Midland Road. The busy shunting engines seemed to be forever on the move, inciting a regular cacophony of buffers, protesting at the sudden acceleration and impacted stops. Along the mainlines (four tracks through Walsall), there was a constant procession of local passenger, mineral and goods trains. All these trains and the connections and crossings to both goods yards were regulated by the signalman in No.1 signal box, who would regularly work an eight-hour shift without a break, which made huge demands on stamina and concentration – just one example of how railway companies demanded maximum sustained effort, for ungenerous wages. We will witness this again as the men's stories unfold.

Walsall Station was always a place of intense activity and included passenger and parcel traffic until the early 1950s, when increased road transport bought about a decline of railway revenue and activity. This was a complete reversal of the railway's almost total dominance for moving freight, and had been witnessed a century before when the railways took business away from the canal network in much the same way. Perhaps the most homely part of Walsall Station was the now-demolished oak-lined concourse which was always warm in winter and resounded to the constant noise of feet on the move. It was a friendly, inviting, semicircular-shaped area which shouted quality and solidity, giving the passengers confidence in the system, denied to modern 'customers' who embark from a modern 'bus-shelter' station. The heftily built booking-office grills had figures behind them that you only knew by their faces; they had no bodies or legs. The cast-iron Nestlé and Cadbury chocolate machines always seemed to deliver superior tasting chocolate than similar products purchased from elsewhere. There was always a friendly ticket collector sitting on a high padded leather stool looking down the long downward-sloping passage leading to the five platforms, the passage sides festooned with hundreds of enamel advertising signs along its length to catch the eyes of the thousands of passengers who used it daily to access their trains. The warmth of the concourse hit you as you passed through the iron and glass canopy. There would be a pleasing greeting from a railway

Left: Walsall station with Stephenson Loco Society special. W.A. Camwell, who organised the tour, is talking to the driver in 1963. There is an ex-LNWR signal and architecture of Webb design. The fireman with his back to camera is Ray Churchill who is still driving steam specials in 2006! (Jack Haddock Collection)

Opposite: Jack Haddock on 23 April 2006 next to the sign erected on Mill Lane nature reserve which depicts various aspects of the site's use over the centuries. (R. Selvey)

company welcoming you, with a foretaste of the piping hot steam-heated carriages, especially on a cold winter's day. Today the station is reached through a redundant corner of the Saddlers centre (a giant shopping mall), or via a soulless sterile passage from a side street (Station Street). Modern, functional and characterless, its lack of inspiration almost gives the impression that passengers should use other transport. At least in hindsight, we can remember the solidity in the building in the age of steam and the durability of its motive power.

Owing to my constant involvement with Walsall's railway life from 1933 to the present, I felt bound, even impelled, to record some of the recent history, lived out daily by our local railwaymen. It has been an honour and pleasure to have been able to interview, and record on audio tape, many retired railwaymen, and to photograph in both black and white and colour from Walsall Station, Ryecroft Junction and the ex-North Western and Midland goods yard. The sight of a railwayman with his loaf-shaped tin box walking to his work or going off duty was a sight familiar to Walsall citizens at any time during the twenty-four hours of the day, but now seems to have completely disappeared. With punctuality and reliability a byword throughout the industry, books on the lives of railwaymen seldom, if ever, mention the unseen input of wives and families of railwaymen, who must have had the patience of Job to put up with the atrocious anti-social hours of work demanded by the shift system, the irregular mealtimes and handwashing of heavy overalls before the days of washing machines. They have always been solidly behind the worker of the family, and have understood his employer's demands and the complexity of his trade. Most railwaymen I have known have had happy and successful marriages and raised contented families. These women behind their men must be remembered, for

without their background help to drivers, firemen, signal men, traffic and permanent way staff and all other workers too numerous to individually mention, the railway companies would not have been able to sustain a first-class railway service. This book tries to tell the story and history of Walsall's Ryecroft locomotive depot.

Jack Haddock
78, Webster Road
Walsall
April 2006

1

Walsall's Engine Sheds

The first engine shed in Walsall was a small building to house and service the motive power of the South Staffordshire Railway Co. The town of Walsall is situated at the edge of the large industrial conglomeration of South Staffordshire that is known as the 'Black Country', and was the ideal centre of operations for a railway firmly based on the movement of coal and iron. The massive seams of the South Staffordshire coalfield (up to 12ft thick), and the locally available limestone for flux and Midland iron ore, had long been exploited. Manufacturing and complex heavy engineering had proliferated to such a degree that before the dawn of the twentieth century, the South Staffs coalfield was in terminal decline. However, beneath the undulating surfaced Bunter pebble beds of nearby Cannock Chase, extensive resources of 'Black Diamonds' in several workable seams were discovered, but they were thrown down deeper by faulting. If developed, deep mining would be expensive and would need the great financial backing of very wealthy individuals, or the grouping of individuals into limited companies with much financial muscle to develop both mines and an efficient means of moving the coal to customers countrywide.

John Robinson McClean, a director of the South Staffordshire Waterworks Co., was aware that the first deep mine on the Chase was being worked at Chasetown, with the Marquess of Anglesea owning the colliery. Due to the ill health of his Lordship, McClean and Richard Chawner arranged to take over the colliery company, which was soon expanded by the sinking of other collieries in the area. The company thrived and became the South Staffs Colliery Co. which, after expansion and takeover, ultimately owned ten collieries on Cannock Chase. Canal and railway facilities were vital for transportation of the huge amounts of good-quality industrial and household coals produced. The railway arm of the enterprise became the South Staffordshire Railway Co., which expanded quickly south-west to Walsall, the hub of its distribution wheel which saw its products promoted countywide, the South Staffordshire Colliery Co. even having a London office.

South Staffs locomotives were small but adequate for the early years, and a small three-road shed was built in Walsall to house them. Fortunately, two old railway maps, now in the archives section of the Walsall Borough, record the site of the shed in Walsall, no trace of which remains today. This humble beginning, concentrating locomotives in one place for servicing and repair, had two covered roads and a third that was open to the elements. It was situated midway between the Bridgeman Street level crossing and the Bodleys crossing. These crossings were eliminated in the mid-1870s due to the increase in density of traffic on both the road and railway, being replaced by the Bridgeman Street subway beneath the railway, and the Corporation Street over-bridge next to the old Bodleys crossing.

Little or nothing has been left on record of this Walsall shed's early years. The shed's first upgrade after building probably occurred as early as 1852 when the engineer, Richard Trevithick, was instructed to install gas into the shed for lighting. In 1857 the South Staffordshire Railway Co. invited tenders for the erection of a girder base and overhead water tank. A small locomotive turntable at the Bodley's crossing was constructed, but it was only long enough to cater for the needs of the small South Staffordshire locomotives. No coaling stage can be defined from the maps and it must be assumed that the coaling of locomotives was a primitive operation, being hand-coaled from conveniently placed wagons. Water supply was obviously in the hands of the South Staffs Water Co. Plenty of iron was available at Walsall for repair work or fabrication. The shed at Walsall, together with the company's other shed at Wychnor, was sufficient to house and service the early batches of locomotives which were operated. These locomotives were often modified in various ways to keep them in service, and lasted from about 1859 to 1878. One such engine was named *Walsall*, but it cannot be confirmed that it was permanently based in the town.

The railway operations of the company were eventually worked by the mighty L&NWR, and subsequently taken over by that company. North-western influence dominated the scene at Walsall by 1874, when a missive from Mr Francis William Webb required the old Walsall engine shed to be cleared for traffic purposes, and from Crewe came a proposal to build a new engine shed at Cannock Junction – Ryecroft shed.

During the 1870s the L&NWR, under Mr Webb, embarked on a standardisation of railway architecture and structures i.e. engine sheds, stations and signal boxes. By the 1870s Walsall's first engine shed, mentioned above, had become hopelessly outdated, and by 1877 its replacement was under construction on a tightly confined site to the north-east of the town, at Ryecroft Junction. The old South Staffordshire shed was demolished, leaving the area for expansion and a four-track layout through the town which offered flexibility to cope with the anticipated growth in traffic. This reached its zenith during the Second World War and on through the late 1940s and early 1950s.

The old Walsall shed certainly came in useful during its twilight years of operation. A newspaper reference from the *Walsall Observer*, dated 20 March 1875, tells of a fire in the ticket office at Walsall station:

> At about 5.50 on Wednesday morning, John Smith, a wagon examiner in the employ of the L&NWR was going to work at the railway station. He found one side of the ticket office and the adjacent lobby that was for the use of first and second class passengers in flames. The hose was fetched but there was difficulty in getting it to work. A couple of locomotives

> were brought along the line and stationed alongside the office. The water was then taken in bucketfuls from their tanks and poured upon the fire which was soon subdued.

The thought occurs that if the engines from the old Walsall shed had not been readily available nearby, then the station might have been destroyed. Instead it survived to be enlarged, the extra facilities coming into use on 1 November 1883. A fire did consume part of the building, however –on 5 May 1916 the booking hall was destroyed. This was eventually rebuilt and the new booking hall was commissioned on 4 November 1923, this latter rebuilding serving Walsall until final demolition in February/March 1978.

Between 1875 and 1879 the Midland Railway became intergrated into the L&NWR system in the Walsall area. The story begins when the powers under the Walsall, Wolverhampton & Midland Junction Railway Act 1872, were transferred to the Midland Railway by an Act of 30 July 1874; and the Midland line from Water Orton to North Walsall Junction was opened to goods traffic on 19 May and passenger traffic on 1 July 1879. The Walsall & Wolverhampton Line was sold to the Midland Railway by the L&NWR on 1 July 1876, and one month later the Midland Railway began to work a passenger service between Walsall and Wolverhampton, using its own engines and coaches. In 1909 both companies became reciprocal users of the line.

Such was the pressure on the railway infrastructure during the 1870s, it was decided to quadruple the railway line from the north at Ryecroft Junction to the south at Pleck Junction. From Ryecroft to Pleck all the bridges were rebuilt. A bridge that also spanned the Fordbrook River replaced the two level crossings (North Street and Portland Street) at Ryecroft. This was called Butts Bridge, named after the local district. Bridges were also erected at Littleton Street, St Pauls Street and Park Street, the latter being Walsall's main shopping thoroughfare. Additional running lines were laid at Walsall Station, but it was not really enlarged until 1 November 1883, with the L&NWR and Midland Railway operating their own systems. Between Walsall Station and Pleck Junction, vast new construction took place. On the up side of the line the Midland Railway had acquired the Walsall Lammas lands, a large meadow which incorporated the Walsall Racecourse. The racecourse was closed and the Midland Railway built sidings for its own goods traffic on the site. On the down side of the line the old South Staffordshire Railway engine shed had been demolished and the L&NWR constructed sidings on the site. Level crossings were replaced by Bridgman Street subway and the Corporation Street Bridge. On the up side, between Corporation Street and the new Pleck Bridge, the Midland Railway constructed a three-road engine shed. On 1 July 1879 the first Midland Railway passenger and goods trains from Water Orton ran into Walsall. The two railway companies serving Walsall remained separate entities until the 1923 grouping, when the L&NWR and the Midland Railway became part of the LMS.

2

Walsall Midland Railway Engine Shed, New Mills

Although this book is largely concerned with the L&NWR engine shed at Ryecroft, we cannot ignore the old Midland Railway shed, which was opened in 1880 and closed on 2 September 1929 as part of the rationalisation that followed the 1923 grouping. The locomotives allocated there were transferred to Ryecroft, Bescot and Saltley sheds after closure. We will begin by describing the old Midland shed before describing the longer-lived L&NWR shed.

It would be fair to say that this very efficient and clean engine shed has by now been practically forgotten. Some ex-Midland railwaymen, however, talk with pride and loyalty about the Midland Railway administration in Walsall, including ex-Midland Railway fitter Gerald Rigby, of 79, Camden Street, Walsall. He was aged seventy-seven when his reminiscences were recorded. He started work as an apprentice fitter at Saltley shed, having managed to get a job by virtue of his father's position as shed foreman at Walsall's New Mills shed. His father, unfortunately, died suddenly in 1918 and young Gerald was granted a transfer to Walsall's Midland shed for domestic reasons. Walsall's Midland shed was part of the Birmingham district, shed code 3, where Saltley was the major depot and Gerald often had to spend periods of time at Saltley or Derby (headquarters of the Midland Railway), in the various engine fitting and maintenance departments. One of his many memories concerns the Midland engines waiting for a road onto the mainline to take up a duty. He remembers the drivers making a special whistle by the Midland signal box, that sounded almost like 'I want to come out on the mainline', and recalls them having to wait for the L&NWR to give permission.

Gerald worked at Walsall Midland shed until the railway grouping of 1923 and did not leave until the shed finally closed in 1925. After a spell of fitting at Saltley, again he applied for a transfer to Bescot to be nearer home. Working as a fitter in an L&NWR shed on their engines led Gerald to learn quickly that the L&NWR was, in fact, somewhat inferior in certain departments compared to various Midland Railway standards of engine maintenance and construction. A standard joke in early days between ex-Midland and L&NWR staff working together was, 'The Midland Railway is 100 years behind the

Walsall Midland shed in use as carriage sidings in 1960, with loco 45593 passing light engine. (Jack Haddock Collection)

times, but the L&NWR is 300'. After working at Bescot for some time Gerald came to the conclusion that Walsall's Midland shed was better laid out and had been worked to a much cleaner system than either Ryecroft or Bescot sheds. Possessing only three running roads, it was complete with a blacksmith's shop, a carpenter's shop and a shop with a furnace for drying sand and heating the very neat and clean administration offices. A high chimney rose from this furnace and, nearby on the roof, was a huge water tank. Passengers on local passenger trains passing the Midland shed in high summer have seen shed staff sitting round the perimeter of this water tank taking advantage of the sheds facility for a free dip during their meal break.

A hand-operated turntable was provided, plus a Midland incline stage, which enabled the shed staff to load coal direct from coal wagon to tender. It was a large building that provided a certain amount of protection from the elements. Cleaning in the engine shed was carried out with the utmost pride. The Midland Railway practice of providing drip trays under all engines in the shed was faithfully carried out and all engines left the shed in a very clean condition. The main entrance for staff arriving for duty was over a small bridge crossing the Fordbrook at a point in Wednesbury Road opposite the present-day Bescot Crescent. Alongside this brook were the railwaymen's allotments, rented to the men by the company. Well-laid-out flowerbeds were placed under the office windows, and there was also a sight you would not normally associate with an engine shed – a large goldfish pond. This pleasant view was no doubt intended for passengers on passing trams!

Gerald Rigby recalls that the mainstay of Walsall's allocation working the local Midland passenger trains were the small but efficient and popular Johnson 0-4-4 tank engines, Nos 1249, 1250 and 1251, plus the larger 0-6-4 tank engines, Nos 2036, 2037 and 2038.

These locomotive worked the passenger services to Wolverhampton via North Walsall or via Pleck, in conjunction with the L&NWR and the main passenger train duty to Birmingham New Street via Water Orton. The 0-4-4 tank engines were usually at work on the Wolverhampton trains, leaving the more powerful 0-6-4 tank engines to handle the heavier trains over the gradients to Birmingham. On arrival in Birmingham New Street, the Walsall-based engines and crews would work through to Redditch and Evesham before returning to Walsall. The only other local passenger service was the thrice-daily, each-way service between Aldridge and Brownhills, allocated to Saltley shed and usually worked by a Midland Johnson Class 2 or Class 3 0-6-0 goods engine. The freight engine allocation for Walsall Midland shed was about six of the Johnson 0-6-0 Class 2 and 3 tender engines, plus two of the Johnson 0-6-0 Class 1 tank engines that were used for shunting, No.1690 being at Walsall for most of its life. It was affectionately known as 'Jacko'. Other Midland engines to be seen in Walsall were the magnificent Johnson 4-2-2 bogie singles and Johnson Class 2 and Class 3 4-4-0 passenger engines. The Class 3 tender engines from Walsall Midland shed had no rest on summer Sundays; they were used for short-distance excursions, mostly to Sutton Park and often with a nine-coach load. The local Sunday schools and various town organisations, including those from the Wolverhampton area, made regular use of these excursions, often making group reservations. Senior citizens I have spoken to who are members of St Peter's Parish church in Stafford Street, Walsall, can remember the annual summer treat which began with a walk up to North Walsall station, to join their train to Sutton Park. The price of a return fare for children was *6d*.

By the early hours of the morning, Walsall Midland shed would not be too busy. One recollection of night duty, as Gerald Rigby remembers, was the regular visit of the police foot patrol to sample a mug of tea or cocoa from the small mess room at the shed. When PC Dudley Edwards of the local constabulary arrived at the shed, he would fill up the nearest tin with tea or cocoa, irrespective of it being stone cold or red hot, and would down it with one gulp. He would then doze on a hard wooden and uncomfortable bench leaving instructions to be woken in time for his liaison with his sergeant at 4 a.m. by the crossroads of Wednesbury Road and Corporation Street.

Within a few years of the 1923 railway grouping, the economies that were being made included the closure of the Midland shed and the staff were re-allocated to various local sheds within the newly formed LMS. They were transferred to Saltley, Bescot and Ryecroft. The steam engines stationed at Walsall Midland shed gradually dwindled in summer, but it was not until 2 September 1925 that the shed finally closed. Most of the engines went to Ryecroft. Surprisingly, the instructions to remove the old turntable were not issued until 23 October 1935. During the 1930s, the LMS put the closed Walsall Midland shed to use as a carriage maintenance facility with its outside network of lines used to accommodate (mostly) sets of excursion stock, of up to twelve coaches. Interestingly, during the Second World War the building was used as a wireless store. In 1969 the old Midland shed was demolished, although it was still in sound condition. Its demolition did not cause any comment or enthusiasm – a pity really, because it had some architectural value, but I do not think many citizens of Walsall ever missed it; in fact, some I talk to today do not know it ever existed.

3

L&NWR Ryecroft Engine Shed

Ryecroft shed was a twelve-road, typical red brick L&NWR construction with a saw tooth 'Northlight' roof, numbered 9 by the L&NWR. Originally, wooden doors were fitted to all roads and lasted throughout the L&NWR era. However, a series of mishaps caused the removal of doors in the 1930s, by then being operated by the LMS as its shed 3C. Shed roads were numbered from the Mill Lane side, which was situated in the Butts district of Walsall.

Roads 1 and 2 only extended two thirds of the shed length, allowing room for the sand furnace, two bunkers for coal, sand drying and other shed installations plus offices. An outside siding ran along the shed beside the sand furnace, a hole in the shed wall with hinged wooden doors enabling a van to draw alongside to facilitate unloading. In winter the sand drying room was a welcome haven for shed staff illicitly escaping from the rigours of the cold. Roads 3 to 9 ran the full length of the shed, with all roads having pits, that of road 9 being deeper to enable running repairs to locomotives to be made with greater ease. The bottom side of road 9 had a set of pulley blocks attached to the main roof, the set-up based on pillars to enable engines side tanks to be removed. With an old bent railway line loosely bolted to the pillars and drilled at various lengths, pulley blocks could be attached for use at varying angles. Roads 10 and 11 were also full length, with a set of hydraulic 'sheerlegs' enabling locomotives to be lifted for wheel and axle box maintenance on road 11. Road 12 was shortened to house the 'sheerlegs'. Adjoining this general service area, a small shed housed a single-cylinder steam engine coupled to a hydraulic water pump, from which ran pipes to the lifting legs. With a locomotive conveniently parked at the end of road 12, steam could be piped to the single-cylinder engine for lifting purposes. The long, straight road shed always provided problems for the efficient stabling of locomotives. For the shift foreman concerned, a complexity of light and heavy repairs, boiler washout routines and tube replacements, with locomotives for short or extended periods of occupancy, required careful planning and tight work schedules.

Pits were drained by gravity into the nearby Fordbrook, but there was little fall on the system and it worked well only when the brook was at low level. After continuous rainfall

Shed view from Mill Lane with 5004, clearly showing the original Webb-designed 'Saw Tooth' roof, 1937. (Harry Russell)

Ivatt Class 2 loco 41224 passing Ryecroft with a Rugeley to Birmingham local, 1955. (Barry Creswell)

or heavy thunder storms, the brook in spate conditions reversed the flow, the pits then became water-logged, causing considerable discomfort to the fitters. Should high brook levels coincide with springtime, then frogs and toads could invade the depot in their hundreds, subsequently finding their way into mess rooms, offices, and staff coat pockets, not always accidentally.

Shed view across the Cannock line in 1950, just prior to modernisation. (Stanley Webb)

The primitive toilet facility at the depot was at the rear of the building near the spoil hill known as the Ryecroft Alps. The installation consisted of a wooden shed with a pole across three large buckets and no privacy. A shed labourer had the unpleasant task of emptying the contents weekly by digging a hole in the field opposite (then railway land) to bury the contents. This unhygienic duty was paid an extra 10*s* a week, the job being known to Ryecroft men as 'the shite shunt'. This state of affairs continued until better provision was included in the rebuilding programme in 1952.

Running the length of the rear of the shed were the stores, blacksmith's shop and mess room, with, further to the Mill Lane side of the shed, the clerk offices and booking-on office with its roster board in the corner. Also at the rear end of the shed was the drinking water fountain, this water coming from the loco water tank as no piped household supply was available. When the line from Wychnor was opened (South Staffordshire Railway) the South Staffs Waterworks Co. put in pipes by the trackside from near Lichfield to supply water to the Black Country and Dudley, this water being tapped for the Ryecroft Depot. The piped water and sanitation improvements of the 1952 programme brought Ryecroft belatedly up to the hygiene standards expected in the twentieth century.

The inside of the shed was generally kept clean, as was the area around the outside running tracks, but the Second World War and its enforced manpower shortage brought a general decline in maintenance standards. Outside installations maintained by Ryecroft fitters were the coaling stage, turntable, ash pit and water columns. The L&NWR loco coaling provision was the usual ramp and platform affair, allowing wagons of coal to be higher than the locomotive's tender or bunker, thus allowing gravity hand coaling. The coaling stage was completely covered by a large water storage tank, gravity feeding the

View of coal plant from ash disposal lift with loco 5417, 1936. (Joe Parr)

shed's two water columns. Although covered by the tank, coaling was a hard and dirty job for the labourers, who worked a three-shift system. This was doubly so in the winter months when bitter cold added to the damp and draft at this location. Ryecroft and other local sheds tried to upgrade facilities in the 1930s, by seeking aid via a Government scheme to create work for the unemployed. The real need for a mechanical coaling system for the larger modern locomotives, with their bigger appetites for coal, forced the Government to put out tenders to industry for mechanical loading facilities. The plan was to select the best designs for building as trial units. A design for a reinforced concrete plant, a development in its infancy in those days, was deemed best for the heavy-duty nature of the coaling activity. Coal was elevated in trucks to be stored in a bunker, to be tapped off at tender top level. The design skills of the Wantage Engineering Co. from Wantage in Berkshire were chosen, their more normal engineering expertise consisting of dock and wharf facilities for the trawling and deep-sea fishing industry. Installation of the plant took about twelve months, the design concept incorporating an ungainly system of iron counterbalance weights to raise a 12-ton load of locomotive coal to the platform. The plant proved troublesome, the guarantee clause of the Wantage Engineering Co. often being invoked to rectify the many teething problems encountered. With modification, the handover day to the LMS saw many officials and departmental staff arriving at Ryecroft to assess its capabilities.

The plant was working well but some months later a manpower shortage arose due to sickness and holidays, and the depot's steam raiser was drafted in to assist. His inexperience with the plant caused an unfortunate accident. In the act of lowering an empty wagon back down, the steady action came to a stop a few inches from rail level, and to release the system the temporary operator put the control into ascent mode. With the heavy counterbalance weights intended to take a loaded wagon up, the empty wagon shot into the air with great force, fracturing the concrete structure of the plant and rendering it useless. Very extensive and time consuming rebuilding was required. Having handed over the plant to the LMS, the Wantage Co. was not interested or available to assist. It was left to Ryecroft fitter Frank Rigby to dismantle the crushed wagon, clear the concrete

Relief Pines Express passing Ryecroft behind loco 5417 showing the collapsed coal plant as described by fitter Frank Rigby in the text, 1937. (Harry Russell)

debris and get the counterbalance system back into working order until a firm could be found to undertake the rebuilding of the coaling plant. With little experience of concrete engineering available, the Danish firm of Beerham & Partners Ltd acquired the renewal tender, the results of their expertise lasting until it was rendered obsolete in 1957 when the shed closed for steam operations. The tower was demolished along with all other installations in 1958 to enable Ryecroft to operate as a servicing shed for the new diesel multiple unit fleet.

Ryecroft had two turntables during the lifetime of the shed. The original, a manually operated L&NWR design, lasted until 1935. Larger locomotives such as the 'Prince of Wales' and 'Claughton' classes were too large to use the original turntable. An 'Experiment' would fit the old turntable with about an inch to spare at each end. The larger and more modern 'Stanier' power classes 5, 5XP and 6P had to be turned by using the ex-Midland/North Walsall triangle, until a new 60ft-diameter, vacuum-operated turntable was installed in 1936. Upgrading of the ash disposal facilities to include a pit, and skip elevation to tip into ash wagons was undertaken around the same time, making disposal less physical but still a filthy and unenviable task.

Lighting at Ryecroft shed was, until 1957, supplied by the local gasworks. The railway company came to an arrangement with the gasworks for free gas, in exchange for free transport to Walsall of coal purchased for gas production. In this situation of trade and barter, the LMS thought it obviously had the best deal, as it had dozens of coal trains operating through Walsall every day, and what difference did an extra 50 or 100 tons of coa,l hauled unpaid, make anyway. Towards the end of operations at Ryecroft, however, perhaps the gas company had the last laugh. Many gas-lit installations were broken up and not replaced, or were deemed pretty useless and let go into disrepair, leaving only a few key areas of the shed reasonably lit. Larger areas of the yard were without light and gas supply, a gas works dream as coal kept being delivered.

The constricted site of the shed was hemmed in by the Cannock branch on one side, and the Lichfield and Water Orton lines on another. To the rear were the spoil heaps excavated and piled high for the establishment of the shed, nicknamed the 'Alps', and the

45680 on turntable after working into Walsall on the Pines Express, 1960. (Jack Haddock Collection)

Above: One of the last views of Ryecroft's steam allocation, in 1956, prior to conversion to a diesel multiple-unit shed. (Barry Cresswell)

Opposite: L&NWR-built Ryecroft Junction signal box, 1954. Note the small signal arm below the gantry, used when light engines arrived on shed. (Roger Shenton)

elevated Lichfield Road Junction to North Walsall line. This formed the third leg of a triangle of lines, meaning light engine movements on and off shed were always a source of friction between Ryecroft shed control and the two duty signal men at Ryecroft signal box. Entrance to the shed was by a spur off the Cannock branch, a small L&NWR type hut being sited almost at the junction, which acted as the 'ringing-off' hut where permission to leave the shed was obtained from the signal box. With light engines for the shed, the signal man set his signals for the operation and controlled a button press which sounded a bell on shed to alert the duty shed turner, to make sure there was a clear road for the arrival, so as not to hamper the flow of local passenger services and the intense freight and coal operations interspersed between them. Smooth operation demanded an amicable working arrangement between box and shed. Looking back it still seems amazing that the large number of locomotive movements on and off the shed during a twenty-four-hour period, could go so smoothly in general, from so constricted a site. Locomotives regularly came into home base from many directions at the same time.

4

Ryecroft Shed – Running Staff Organisation

In a typical twenty-four-hour period of operation, some 200 locomotive movements, either arriving or departing, could be expected. It was not only 3C's allocation that was involved, but also locomotives from considerable distances away working into the Walsall area. Along the winding Mill Lane and over the substantial bridge covering the four tracks to Sutton Coldfield and Lichfield, could be seen a constant movement of men, either reporting for duty or returning home after their shift had ended. This sight occurred throughout the day and night.

With an allocation of about fifty-five locomotives, approximately 300 jobs were available at the shed, their organisation being governed by a system that needed careful planning to produce an efficient use of the human resources available. The shed master was responsible for the planned use of motive power, by the establishment of a system of working pools or links to man, service and maintain the prime movers and to allocate and match such resources to the movement of passengers and freight. A core knowledge of daily services was obviously essential, but seasonal excursions and special needs could result in operating problems. At these times both men and machines had to be 'hired out and bought in', to give flexibility to operations throughout the wider Midlands area. This was done under the oversight of a central control. The shed master at Ryecroft was assisted by a shed foreman, who was in charge of three shift foremen overseeing depot activities in each twenty-four-hour period.

Footplate crews at Ryecroft were assigned duties in four passenger links: two freight links; a shunting link; a double trip link and a special link. Each link could be considered as a specialist pool, covering a specific aspect of motive power provision. The progression of both firemen and drivers was based on experience and promotion within a link, or progression from one link to another. The top link for firemen was No.1 goods link, and the top link for senior experienced drivers was No.1 passenger link, these men being passed for long-distance work by knowing signalling arrangements and routes up and down the country. Their route knowledge was vital for summer seasonal, excursion and special traffic. This seeming anomaly in seniority was brought about by the fact that most

Ryecroft Webb 1P 2-4-2T loco 6668 tackling the Cannock Chase gradient from Rugeley to Hednesford on a local passenger train to Birmingham, 1936. (John Bucknall Collection)

firemen in the No.1 goods link were qualified as 'passed firemen', and qualified to drive whilst awaiting a regular position. If they were needed to drive it did not disrupt the organisation of the passenger link. The temporary loss of a passed fireman to a driver's post could be filled by a 'passed cleaner' (qualified to fire) on a local goods service to gain experience, but to put such an operative on passenger work with its tight schedules, demanding advanced firing skills, could be to put him out of his depth with consequent loss of time and disruption of the service. A further consequence was that some firemen and drivers in the No.1 goods link could possibly be of similar age.

5

The Passenger Links

The No.1 passenger link consisted of twelve duty turns, the driver and fireman operating the same trains daily for a week, then working down a rota for the twelve weeks which usually involved working day and night shifts. The three other passenger links were of either ten or eight weeks' rotation depending on traffic requirements. One of these was known as the 'class 3 link', using the shed's allocation of Fowler 3P 2-6-2Ts (and sometimes 'Stanier's' taper boiler version) on the local passenger services radiating from Walsall throughout the West Midlands. The Fowlers were never noted as brilliant steamers, normally being allocated to the lighter jobs. This fact was evident in the career of Ken Horan, when a 3P 2-6-2T was selected by the shed's inspector when examining Ken's firing competence as a cleaner, to graduate to 'passed cleaner' status. The inspector travelled with him on the foot plate for the best part of a day. Perhaps the theory was if you can make a Fowler steam you can successfully fire anything. The Stanier counterpart was little better on its introduction, it, too, suffering from drafting problems which ultimately led to a few being fitted with larger boilers.

Passenger Train Working – The Class 3 Fowler Tanks 1930–1948

In 1930 Pyecroft shed was allocated some of the new Fowler parallel-boiler Class 3 tank engines, to cope with the heavier local passenger workings. At first the Ryecroft crews thought they were an improvement, with regard to maintaining timekeeping, but they soon found out they were little better than the '1P' Webb tanks they were set to replace. The Ryecroft fitters had to perform various experiments and modifications to affect some improvements in the class. Their steaming capability was particularly bad. Despite this, these Class 3 tanks became the mainstay of Ryecroft local passenger trains until the advent of the Second World War. Nos 9, 11, 16, 17, 18, 19, 45 and 69 were faithful servants to the local scene for many years. Initially, Nos 10 and 20 were part of the stud, but left quite

Ryecroft-based Fowler Class 3 tank No.9 crossing Cannock Chase with a local train to Birmingham, 1936. (John Bucknall Collection)

soon for service on the Harrow line (London). The Fowler tanks could usually be seen hauling suburban pattern three-coach unit stock, frequently made up to six coaches for rush-hour working. When working these heavier trains their performance certainly left something to be desired, despite the fact that these engines had a high degree of superheat. To try and overcome their problems, permission was given by Crewe for the Ryecroft fitters to experiment with various sized copper rings in the blast pipe, and by all accounts there was some improvement in performance, but on the whole they were not too popular with their crews. One thing crews did appreciate was the comfort of the totally enclosed cab with seats. The Fowler tanks always worked the Birmingham New Street to Rugeley commuter trains, thus putting an end to the reign of the Webb Cauliflowers on this duty. Frequently in mid-winter, for working the first passenger train out of Rugeley at about 6.15 a.m., a Cauliflower had to proceed tender first from Ryecroft across Cannock Chase against a north wind. If there was also driving rain or snow, this was an experience not easily forgotten. Admittedly, the crews on the Cauliflower had the protection of a tarpaulin sheet draped from cab to tender, but the totally enclosed cab on a Class 3 was more than welcome.

Ryecroft shed was also responsible for working the last passenger train of the day from Birmingham New Street to Rugeley. This apparently straightforward job could have its problems. It was booked to leave New Street at approximately 10.45 p.m., and due to arrive at Rugeley having stopped at all stations, at about 11.50 p.m. It then shunted its empty stock and returned light engine to Ryecroft at around 12.30 a.m. The snag about this normal routine passenger was that the train was not allowed to leave New Street station until the last trains from London, Bristol, Derby and Crewe had arrived. This was to enable passengers to make their connection with the Rugeley local. It has been known for some of these long-distance trains to be as much as two hours late. If one was unfortunate enough to be a passenger on one of these occasions, it could be a frustrating wait, especially as these delays more often than not occurred in mid-winter or inclement weather. I well recall one January night in 1938 after a night at the theatre, waiting until about 12.30 a.m., just sitting in the carriage listening to the eerie echoing noises from the vast cavern roof of the old New Street station. Sitting in the coach, half asleep and rather cold, suddenly a nearby engine would blow off steam and a piercing guard's whistle would split the air. One then proceeded to doze again until the porters with their long line of rail trollies came rattling by. At least one envied them, busy about their business and keeping reasonably warm. Each train emerging from the tunnel raised one's hopes, only to be disappointed by yet another mail train, which seemed to abound in the early hours. When the offending train eventually did arrive, within seconds the guard of the local train would appear from nowhere to get your train moving.

If you were one of the passengers on the late express, one tended to think that the local was going to suddenly leave you stranded. So from the express to the local one would hear the general stampede up the steps and over the famous long footbridge at New Street, then down the steps to the old platform 1A. Here the passengers would dive thankfully into the nearest compartment of the waiting local. Then came the relief of hearing the guard's whistle, and the local on the move at last. On alighting at Walsall with its dim and dingy gas lamps, the ticket collector would be in no mood to study the tickets at that late hour. I think if anyone gave him a 'bus ticket' he would probably not have noticed. Speaking of buses immediately brings one memory to mind. If one happened to live any distance from any of the stations en route to Rugeley, it was a case of walking the last part of the journey as the bus services did not wait for the last train to arrive.

Perhaps the highlight of the Class 3 link duties concerns the one occasion that Ryecroft shed actually worked an express passenger train. The routine was to work a train from Birmingham to Stafford via Walsall, and return via Wolverhampton and the Stour Valley line, back to Birminghamham. It began as a straightforward local to Rugeley, giving the crews a break there of some fifteen minutes. It then proceeded to Stafford, calling at Colwich and Milford. After running round the train at Stafford came Ryecroft's moment of glory – to run as an express passenger to Wolverhampton non-stop at approximately 70mph. At Wolverhampton the fireman had to then change the headcode lamps back to local passenger, for an all stations to Birmingham via Dudley Port run. Another important fast local was to work the early-morning train to Stechford, to enable local businessmen to connect with a fast London Express at Stechford. This was, I believe, a routine to help relieve some of the rush-hour congestion at New Street.

In around 1938, Ryecroft was allocated some of the new Class 3 Stanier taper boiler-tank engines, to be drafted into the Class 3 link. It appears from all accounts that these new engines were little better in general performance than their Fowler counterparts. Most Ryecroft drivers and firemen seem to agree that the performance of the Fowler and Stanier Class 3 tank engines was poor. When Ryecroft was eventually allocated the modern Class 4 Stanier tanks, and some of the older Fowler Class 4 tanks during the

Fowler tank 17 crosses Cannock Chase with a Birmingham to Rugeley local. (John Bucknall Collection)

Second World War, they found to their amazement that they had in both a very useful and efficient engine. They proved very popular with crews and maintenance staff alike, and stayed until Ryecroft shed closed for passenger duties in 1957. The Fowler tanks of the Class 3 link disappeared from Ryecroft for good during the war years, most passenger workings being allotted to the new Class 4 link. Some of the Stanier Class 3 tanks did remain at Ryecroft, mainly for working short-distance mail trains and as Midland Road carriage sidings shunters which also included carriage-warming duties. In fact, Nos 40080, 40083, 40129 and 40173 survived until about 1963 on this duty, at that time working from Bescot shed. One of them on this Bescot link was responsible for working the last of two steam-hauled passenger trains through Walsall. These were two local passengers in the evening rush hour from Kynochs at Witton to Brownhills.

From 1957, when Ryecroft closed its doors to steam engines, all local trains manned from Ryecroft shed were worked by the new diesel multiple units then being introduced. Even these modern, clean and appealing trains could not stem the tide of car ownership and use, so it was that – with the exception of the Walsall to Birmingham New Street trains – all local services had ceased operation by 1965. Most were closed under proposals put forward by Dr Beeching, whose task it was to try and bring the railways back to some sort of profitability.

The Pines Express – A Ryecroft and Saltley Contention

The first Walsall station opened in Bridgeman Place in 1847, as, essentially, a local passenger station. Travellers for destinations further afield had to journey to Birmingham and change trains at New Street. A new Walsall station was opened on 9 April 1849 on the present site, when the South Staffordshire Co. opened a line to Wychnor Junction, giving access to the Birmingham–Derby line of the Midland Railway. The L&NWR took over the South Staffordshire system on 1 February 1879 and dominated the area around Walsall until the Midland penetrated to Walsall with a line from Castle Bromwich via Sutton. This increased the volume of traffic through the town so much that the tracks through Walsall had to be quadrupled, and a new station having five platforms and associated bays was built. It relieved the congestion on its opening on 1 November 1883.

At the time of the grouping to form the LMS in 1923, Walsall station was handling almost 1,000 train movements every twenty-four hours. These were mainly mineral, goods trains or light engine movements, but from 5.55 a.m. to 11.45 p.m., some 120 local passenger trains served Walsall. Over the years many day excursions, seaside visits and evening and afternoon excursions to theatres, greyhound, horse and motor-cycling events, in addition to specially chartered trains for work's and social gatherings, also helped the station to become the thriving hub of a densely populated area of intense commerce and trade.

From the summer of 1927, Walsall was host to its only scheduled express train. Both the up and down 'Pines Express' from Manchester to Boumemouth, were booked to stop in the station to change locomotives on Saturdays only. The weekday 'Pines' passed just inside the Walsall boundary along the old Grand Junction line at Bescot on its down journey, but its up pathing was via the Stour Valley line between Birmingham, Dudley Port and Wolverhampton. The Saturday diversion was obviously to reduce pressure on New Street's resources, by eliminating locomotive watering and exchange for fresh engines. High summer weekends in Birmingham New Street were hectic. The up Pines arrived at Walsall via Darlaston Junction, then ran over the Midland to Castle Bromwich and the Camp Hill avoiding line (thus bypassing Birmingham New Street), to continue its journey south. In Bradshaw's timetable it was shown as not to pick up passengers at Walsall, the express on summer Saturdays being invariably full on leaving Crewe. Passengers from Walsall and Birmingham had their own summer special to Bournemouth during the morning. The 'Pines', however, did exchange locomotives in both directions on Saturday at Walsall station. During high-summer weekends, pressure on the service was intense and 'relief' trains had to be run. Either one or two extra trains would run, likewise exchanging locomotives at the station. These extras would usually arrive some half an hour or more later than the main train. 'Pines' engines and reliefs were serviced at Ryecroft shed until 1957, when Bescot took over all steam servicing in Walsall, Ryecroft being designated as a service base for the new diesel multiple unit fleet.

'Pines' engines and crews originated from Longsight shed, Manchester. The guard booked off at Walsall station, resuming his split-shift duty as the engine left Ryecroft (and later Bescot) for the return down leg at about 3.15 p.m. The locomotive that was to take over the 'Pines' was held in Platform 1A at Walsall before the arrival of the up train, men and locomotive being provided by Saltley shed, Birmingham.

On the train's arrival at Platform 1 some very smart work was needed to get the incoming power from Manchester separated from the train and away from the station confines, allowing the waiting locomotive or locomotives to cross the intricate pointwork, couple-up and depart for the south. It was a routine demanding close co-operation from

Pines Express passing Ryecroft with ex-Midland locos 395 and 1013 in charge, 1935. (John Bucknall Collection)

signalmen in Walsall's No.2 and No.3 signal boxes. The allocated time for the operation was ten minutes, and during this time station staff would also be responsible for topping up the water tank of the restaurant car. This time was often bettered for a late arriving train, when a minimum time at rest would be required, allowing the train to pull back time in view of the tight pathing during a hectic summer timetable.

The fact that Saltley provided the locomotives and crews to work the train forward from Walsall, caused frustration and animosity among Ryecroft men. They resented the light engine working involved in both directions for a train which stopped for locomotive substitution in Walsall Station, less than half a mile from their shed. With Saltley men knowing the road to Bath, they were adamant that the job should be theirs, as Ryecroft men would have to be specially trained for that road. This was not strictly true, however, as Ryecroft could produce six drivers familiar with the road by virtue of working trains over the route. These men had been based at the old Walsall New Mills, Midland engine shed, in the Pleck district of Walsall before its closure in 1925.

After a protracted series of Local District Committee meetings, Ryecroft did win a few concessions for working to Bath. Occasionally, owing to peak summer timetable demands, Saltely did have a shortage of locomotives and manpower. Thus in the late 1920s and '30s, Ryecroft was allocated two ex-Midland engines for assistance. From 1931 to 1939 ex-Midland 2-4-0s Nos 8 (later 20008) and 157 (later 20157) came to the depot for double-heading purposes (standard Midland style), but well into the Stainer era they could hardly be considered a blessing. Ryecroft would have settled for a new Stanier Class 5 mixed traffic locomotive which would need no assistance.

The main motive power for the pre-war 'Pines' was the Standard Compound and Johnson 2P 4-4-0s and of course their LMS developments. After the war Stainer Class 5s and Horwich 'Crab' 2-6-0s took over the duty. Ryecroft men did have one working to Bath, a special Manchester–Bournemouth departing from the northern metropolis at about 11 p.m. arriving for a Walsall locomotive change around 1.30 a.m., the train always being referred to unofficially as a 'Pines Express'.

Walsall station was well used by railway observers in the 1930s for summer Saturday operations. Harry Russell still has notes of the following visitors from Longsight shed. His first recollections are of 'Prince of Wales' 4-6-0s, sometimes assisted by a 'Precursor' 4-4-0,

The Pines Express in Walsall station, having exchanged locomotives, is ready to take its load of holidaymakers south at the start of their holidays. (Jack Haddock Collection)

with an occasional 'Experiment' putting in an appearance on the relief services. Some regular performers, however, were:

5606 *Conqueror*
5609 *Hermione*
5635 *Charles Lamb*
5636 *Percy Bysshe Shelley*
5638 *Charles James Lever*
5640 *General Joffre*
5645 *Raymond Poincare*
5670 *Albion*
5688 *Tara* (A 'Tishy' fitted with outside Walschaerts valve gear)
5697 *Richard Cobden*
5702 (Painted red for a time)
5709, 5727, 5775, 5831, 5835, 5841 and 5844

The following 'Claughton' Class 4-6-0s were also quite regular, being displaced from their former front-line express locomotive status by 'Royal Scot' 4-6-0s:

5914 *J. Bruce Ismay*
5922 *Lord Kenyon*
5939 *Clio*
5940 *Columbus*
5967 *Lance Corporal J A Christie V.C.*
5994
6002 *Thalaba*

The following were the larger boilered 5xP 'Claughton' rebuilds:

5908 *Alfred Fletcher*
5910 *J A Bright*
5927 *Sir Francis Dent*
5946 *Duke of Connaught*
5948 *Baltic*
5957
5970 *Patience*
5975 *Talisman*
5986
5993
5999 *Vindictive*
6004 *Princess Louise*
6013
6017 *Breadalbane*
6023 *Sir Charles Cust*

The following new 'Patriot' Class 4-6-0s were used on the service:

5902 *Sir Frank Ree*
5942
5959
5971
6008 *Lady Godiva*

No 'Royal Scot' 4-6-0s appeared on the 'Pines' at Walsall in pre-war days, being kept for heavy north/south mainline service.

The down 'Pines' arrived at Walsall at approximately 3 p.m. and was invariably double-headed. This time the changeover was the principal responsibility of No.2 signal box. When the locomotives that had brought in the train were making their way back to Saltley, an interesting procedure took place at Ryecroft Junction. Ryecroft signal box would turn them up the Walsall to Wolverhampton line to North Walsall Junction. Here they crossed over tracks at the old North Walsall station, to run chimney-first to Lichfield Road Junction and thus chimney-first onwards to Saltley shed. This routine enabled North Walsall signal-box crews a moment of glory, the express engines being a welcome change from passenger tank locomotives, Midland Class 2 and 3 tender freight engines and 'Super D' 0-8-0s. These classes were the standard power for the stretch of line. From 1936 Stanier Class 5s, Horwich 'Crabs' and the occasional new 5xP 'Jubilee' Class came onto the scene, sometimes headed by a Compound or Class 2 4-4-0. I recall a memorable visit to North Walsall Junction of an immaculate ex-works 'Jubilee' 5557 named *New Brunswick*, coupled to a highly cleaned Compound 4-4-0 after their 'Pines Express' duty.

In the final years of 'Pines' operation at Walsall, Stanier Class 5s and 'Brittania' Pacifics were used on the service, along with rebuilt 'Royal Scots' and rebuilt 'Patriot' Class locomotives. As dieselisation progressed, 'Peak' Class 1-Co-Co-1 diesel electrics undertook some services, and I recorded D15, D114, D151 and D153 as motive power for this fascinating train.

During electrification work at Wolverhampton High Level, the train was re-routed away from Walsall, running from Crewe via Shrewsbury to reach Wolverhampton Low Level over Great Western tracks. Motive power was substituted there, and a Stafford Road Castle performed the honours, running with a 'Pines Express' headboard. It is thought this diversion only lasted for a short time so photographs with headboard are extremely rare.

The train gained its name from the pine forests of Hampshire, through which it would pass on its way to Bournemouth. It remains notable as the only 'named' train booked to stop at Walsall on a regular basis.

Days of The Dudley Dashers

These were the first passenger trains to run from Walsall to Dudley on 1 May 1850. Unfortunately, there appears to be no record of the type of locomotives or stock that worked the line. Information relating to passenger services from Walsall prior to the 1900s seems to be almost non-existent. In post-1923 grouping days, a feature of the Dudley service was the existence of a small engine shed at Dudley, effectively a sub-shed of Ryecroft 3C. Ryecroft had an allocation of five or six Webb 1P 2-4-2T locomotives for working local push-and-pull fitted auto trains, one of these being allocated to the services from Dudley to the mainline station at Dudley Port, an interesting split-level complex which also had the canal as a close neighbour. The drivers and firemen were local Dudley men operating the five-minute shuttle to 'Port', with the locomotive operating about seventeen hours per day. At about midnight it retired to its little shed to be cleaned, oiled and prepared by a Ryecroft cleaner who had arrived on the last train from Walsall. Return for him would be on the first train the following morning. He was also responsible for calling up both driver and fireman in readiness for the first service at 5.45 a.m. Retired Ryecroft driver Walter Franklin recalls his work on the 'Dasher' during the First World War, stating that its driver lived in the vicinity of Dixons Green while the fireman came from Tividale. One can imagine the long walk around Dudley at 4 a.m., especially in fog or heavy snow, before returning to the shed to raise steam for the little Webb's first duty. With its lightweight train, the engine managed, even with its small bunker, to do the job without having to supply coal to the small Dudley shed. A daily exchange of locomotives took place each afternoon, the 'Dudley Dasher' locomotive then heading a Dudley to Walsall passenger, allowing a servicing visit to Ryecroft where the bunker would again be piled high with enough coal for the next twenty-four hours. Over the years the 'Dasher' averaged some twenty-five trips between Dudley and the 'Port' daily, its function to meet every express (and most local trains) calling at the high-level platforms. The journey was repetitive, but the journey from the low-level line to Dudley and into the high-level platforms was made up a curving incline, and the line also had to cross the nearby canal to boot. Another duty undertaken by the locomotive off the 'Dasher', was to run down to the nearby Pahethorpes sidings, to convey the well-known four- and six-wheeled sausage vans for transfer to Dudley. From here, GWR trains would deliver to destinations on their territory. The locomotive returned empties to the factory, and then became reunited with its stock for more to-ing and fro-ing.

In the days before the First World War, another local train was worked between Wednesbury Town and Dudley Port. This ran via Princes End, Tipton, with some four journeys a day being made. Mainly for the benefit of passengers arriving at Wednesbury Central (GWR), the service enabled them to reach Black Country destinations along the Stour Valley L&NWR line. These trains were always worked by Webb 'Gadget' 0-6-2Ts, the locomotive running round its coaches at Dudley Port and Wednesbury, not working on the push-pull principle. Most of this locomotive's time was spent shunting around Wednesbury Town goods yard. In 1916 this passenger service was curtailed, probably as a wartime economy.

The older type of Webb 2-4-2Ts had 4ft 6in driving wheels and were fitted with a rod-operated regulator, but in LMS days the company introduced the improved version with 5ft 6in driving wheels and vacuum-operated regulator control. This allowed for 'push-pull' operation, the driver in one direction operating from the front carriage of the train with the fireman alone on the footplate. A story related by an ex-Ryecroft driver tells of one 1930s journey. Having just left Great Bridge station in propelled mode, a local policeman saw the spectacle and reported it as a runaway train. The engine, being low on coal, had forced the fireman to crawl into the bunker to move coal forward, so the astonished policeman viewed a totally empty footplate. The outcome of this report at the police station went unknown, but there must have been some very red faces.

Black Country railwaymen nicknamed the push-pull units 'Motor Choppers', but to the locals they were always 'Dudley Dashers'; I recall the name 'Dudley Back Dasher' also being used. Until the improvement of bus and motor car transport in the early 1950s, this train was a vital means of transport for thousands of factory workers travelling from Walsall to Black Country industrial areas. The trains were also a useful transport link from Walsall, for theatre lovers journeying to matinée and evening performances at Dudley Hippodrome for variety, pantomine and other entertainment. The journey, including stops, took about twenty minutes. This is difficult to achieve with a modern car today, and certainly much better than a forty-minute bus schedule.

By 1950, Walsall's allocation of Webb 5ft 6in 2-4-2Ts had been reduced to four, 6689, 6701, 6742 and 6743 having done yeoman service on the push-pull trains, which from then were gradually handed over to the newer and more efficient Ivatt 2-6-2Ts, 41224 and 41279 being well remembered. Occasionally Fowler 3P and Stanier 4P tanks worked heavier three- to six-coach trains at rush-hour times, giving greater seating capacity. The Dudley line, in later years of steam, saw some heavy trains to the zoo and hippodrome originating from as far afield as Lincoln, Wakefield, Nottingham and the South Yorkshire towns, which resulted in some very interesting locomotive types on Bank Holidays and Sundays. Ryecroft men often acted as pilot men on these duties but, frequently, the services were re-manned at Burton-On-Trent. Burton crews were able to work straight through to Dudley as they were familiar with the route, via their freight workings to the Black Country. Perhaps the most spectacular of 'foreign' locomotive types were the

LNWR loco 2126 with Ryecroft shed staff, *c.*1920. This is one of the Webb-designed locos used on the 'Dudley Dasher'. (Alan Price)

Thompson BI 4-6-0s seen on twelve-coach trains, or K3 2-6-0s (both types visiting from the Eastern region of British Railways). Stanier Jubilees, Black 5s and Horwich-built Fowler 'Crabs' from Burton shed also made numerous appearances. Ryecroft diesel multiple unit services worked on the line after withdrawal of steam in 1957, but the line soon closed for passenger services, falling victim to the post-Beeching cuts in 1965.

Reminiscing on my journeys from Walsall to Dudley as a small lad, I well remember the stationmaster's whistle as the train departed from Walsall. Within seconds we were passing 'Bodley's' and the Midland sidings filled with wagons, with various private owners names prominently painted on their sides. There was always the urgent staccato exhaust of busy shunting engines. Passing under Corporation Street bridge, on the right was the District Engineer's yard and Permanent Way Department. On the left was the fairground, where at various times throughout the year one could see Pat Collins's fair in all its bustle and glory, its gleaming showman's engines at work on top of the bank next to the railway. The engines carried evocative names like *Goliath*, *Dreadnought* and *Emperor*, the ultimate muscle machines on the road in the age of steam.

Passing under the New Mills bridge at the Pleck, passengers would smell the old Walsall gas works; carriage windows would then be pulled up by the solid slotted leather strap, just in time to ward off the scented aroma of Bescot sewerage works. By this time the push-pull train was probably travelling at 50 to 60mph, arriving in Wednesbury Town in about five minutes. Here, the very pleasant aroma of freshly-cut timber greeted the passengers as the train came to rest adjacent to the Walsh Graham timber yard and sawmills. Looking out of the snug compartment as the train bid farewell to Wednesbury across its guarded level crossing, passengers could often catch a glimpse of gleaming GWR locomotives in their Brunswick green livery, their chocolate and cream coaches passing across the bridge over the Dudley line. In four minutes the train would be approaching Great Bridge, passing over two canal bridges of the Birmingham Canal Navigation Co., with a view of horse-drawn coal boats and tugs, with traffic for the railway/canal interchange basin. Great Bridge had a large and very busy goods yard close to its station. From here operated a fleet of horse-drawn delivery carts and wagons, busily plying their trade, in concert with the new Scammel mechanical horse-articulated units (set to replace the horse-drawn units), and a few railway-owned Albion heavy lorries that served the multitude of Black Country factories.

The train then left Great Bridge for the very short three-minute run to Dudley Port, between a maze of factories and terraced houses. On arrival the train waited for four or five minutes allowing passengers to interchange with the upper platforms. On the final short trip to Dudley Town station and on past the Palethorpes sausage factory, passengers could catch sight of Dudley Castle, a sentinel on its wooded hill, before pulling into the station. Here, the veteran Webb engine would find a companion as a GW auto train was encountered with its usual pannier tank, so typical of this era. On ascending the steps to alight on Castle Hill, one would be confronted by ranks of Midland Red SOS buses, around the extensive garaging facility opposite the station. One could not imagine that these distinctive buses and their successors would one day kill off the short-distance local trains, but with the help of the motor car, they succeeded. The era of the local train had to come to an end, but I for one am glad to have lived in the age of steam-hauled transport, to have known its drivers, firemen and associated railway staff who made this form of transport possible.

Although only a short journey, with vintage locomotives and well-worn, well-mellowed stock passed down to eke out its final years in steam's decline, what an indelible record remains grafted in the memory, as we recall the 'chaff-chaff' of tall chimneys and small engines incongruously refusing to die and providing a service of clockwork reliability throughout a desperate wartime era – only to be followed by the years of severe austerity, rationing and shortage. By comparison, the Ivatt 2MT 2-6-2T locomotives that succeeded them were considered 'superpower' and 'light years' in advance of the Webb era by their crews. With local rail travel in steep decline as private and public road transport wooed the passengers to the concrete and tarmac, the age of elegance and vintage steam travel by rail was lost forever. For the weekly service between Walsall, Dudley and Dudley Port, three locomotives with two-coach units were needed. On the Walsall service in times of extra need, four-coach sets could be used with the locomotive in the middle of the train. For the Dudley Port shuttle service, no more than two coaches were allowed. Spare sets of two coaches were always available for any emergency. Until about 1927, one locomotive and two coaches were stationed at Dudley, its early morning till late at night utilisation making it necessary to have two sets of crew based there. A change in the LMS era then saw stock based overnight at the 'back yard' carriage sidings, adjacent to the 'up fast' relief loop-line in Walsall station. By 1932 the system had diagrammed the working of the three

Another loco used on the 'Dudley Dasher', Webb 2-4-2T 6757 at Ryecroft, in 1950, as modernisation of the shed begins. (Jack Haddock Collection)

sets from Walsall, but for a time the Dudley men still booked on at Dudley. Originally, one set worked the Dudley to Dudley Port shuttles with a Dudley crew. The two locomotives and sets working Walsall to Dudley and return were either Ryecroft or Dudley men. By the early 1930s all crews signed on at Ryecroft, on diagrams worked from Ryecroft. A new diagram appraisal introduced an outing to Dudley, then a period of three to five Dudley port return trips, followed by a return to Walsall, any crew changes being made at Walsall station.

The maintenance of the three push-pull units involved a daily inspection of each unit by a fitter from Walsall Ryecroft shed. Whilst the locomotives had a daily inspection on arrival at the shed, the coaches came under the jurisdiction of the carriage and wagon department, except the forward driving compartments of the sets which were the preserve of the Locomotive Operating department. This entailed the attention of a Ryecroft fitter for a few hours each day. Complete with tools, he would leave the shed on one of the relieving 2-4-2T's making its way to Walsall, allowing the incoming engine to visit Ryecroft for coal, water and servicing. Subsequently, the fitter travelled on each of the push-pull trains for about four hours, this usually taking place in mid-afternoon. During this time, various maintenance checks were carried out, with any necessary adjustments being made as the locomotive waited at the main stations. Any faults found to require major attention were wired through to Walsall station, where a spare set could be substituted. At no time could any Ryecroft men remember any serious delay or disruption of the service – a tribute to the efficient maintenance regimes practiced.

Push-Pull Trains

In order to reduce the need for locomotives to uncouple from their train, run-round and then re-couple, a push-pull method of operation was used on some services. Wolverhampton to Rugeley and Brownhills, including Lichfield on Saturdays, were some of them. Other services were to Dudley and Birmingham.

The modern Ivatt 2-6-2T (Class 2) locomotives were ideal for this sort of work and they were comfortable, roomy on the footplate and looked smart. Before this highly praised type, the venerable L&NWR Webb 2-4-2T (Class 1P) was used and also stood in for the Ivatt when the luxury model was in for repairs. The veterans, which dated back to 1890 and featured Crewe's grand domes and tall chimneys, had become an anachronism in the Stanier and post-Stanier era. They were thought of as uncomfortable by the crews, cramped, extremely hot in the cab and certainly not an oil painting to look at! They were, however, quite robust and economical. One bad feature was the bunker hole from which the fireman shovelled the coal, which was very small. When a large lump became wedged there and the engine was working hard, it became panic stations if it did not yield to the swing of the fireman's coal pick. The firebed would be hungry to be fed, as the best way to fire this L&NWR locomotive was 'light and often'. There was only one way out of this dilemma and that was by opening the large, top door of the bunker and taking the coal by hand to feed the fire, until time would allow the extraction of the offending piece of coal.

Another awkward design feature common to quite a lot of L&NWR locomotives was the small fire-hole ratchet door, which opened inwards at the pull of a lever. The door plate itself acted as a baffle which directed secondary air under the brick-arch. The heat of the firebox sometimes caused the fire-hole-door to warp, making a bad seal when closed. This would make it awkward to fire with a full shovel because the door now drooped downwards.

A typical service would see a two-coach train being propelled to, say, Rugeley, the engine being at the rear with the fireman all alone on the footplate. The driver sat in the cab of the leading coach operating two vacuum valves, one which would work the regulator valve on the outside of the engine smokebox, and the other which applied the brake. On starting away, the fireman received bell signals from the driver and he would open the regulator on the footplate. Initially to a required setting, he would then adjust the valve travel as necessary as the engine gathered speed, by winding up or down the forward and reverse gear to select the right amount of valve cut-off. Although the regulator on the locomotive could, in theory, be left open throughout, the driver and fireman adopted their own method of working. The driver who was in the leading coach would shut off steam when wishing to coast, by destroying the vacuum which operated the regulator valve on the locomotive. In reality, the vacuum-controlled regulator valve often 'blew through' slightly, which meant that a small amount of steam was still being fed to the cylinders, which does not help when trying to stop! It was operationally easier and safer for the fireman to close the regulator valve in the cab when he saw the regulator vacuum gauge needle fall to zero. This indicated that the driver had 'technically' shut off. Although this meant the fireman having to close and open the regulator each time he observed the vacuum gauge needle fall, and when the signal to start was given, it made for a far smoother departure at each station without any surge on starting away. It also lessened the risk of overshooting a station because a small amount of steam was still reaching the cylinders when stopping. None of this 'unofficial technique' is to be found in any operating manual, of course!

On occasions where extra coaches were necessary, the engine would be in the middle of the train and the fireman would be alone on the footplate when travelling in either direction. Because of these extra duties and responsibilities on the push-pull trains (known also as 'motor' or 'auto' trains) the fireman had to be specially examined and passed out by the footplate inspector, which provided another step in the right direction towards becoming a driver.

Ryecroft's Allocation of Webb 2-4-2 Tank Locomotives

With the very intensive local services pre-war, including the specialised 'push-pull' services described above, Ryecroft had a very strong allocation of these small, but extremely useful, L&NWR locomotives. The type was typical Webb: simple, robust, well constructed, good steamers, footsure and economical in operation. The last of the type was withdrawn from Ryecroft duties in the mid-1950s, on the introduction of lvatt 2MT 2-6-2Ts. Although described as cramped and uncomfortable, the type was well liked by operating crews. Easy on service and maintenance, its simplicity was welcomed by fitters and management alike. Below is a listing of the type allocated to the depot over a period of time from 1935 to the end of 2-4-2T allocation. Later transfers are recorded if known.

Number	Sept. 1935	April 1944	Jan. 1948	Sept. 1950	Jan. 1954
6620	3C	Shrewsbury	Swansea	Swansea	-----
6637	3C	Llandudno Jcn	Sutton Oak	-----	
6661	3C	3C	3C	-----	
6664	3C	-----			
6668	3C	-----			
6671	3C	-----			
6679	3C	3C	3C	-----	
6685	3C	3C	-----		
6689	3C	3C	-----		
6701	3C	Rugby	Rhyl	Warrington	-----
6712	Workington	Llandudno Jcn	Rhyl	3C	3C
6742	3C	Crewe	Northampton	-----	
6743	3C	Watford	-----		
6753	3C	Bangor	-----		
6757	Swansea	Swansea	3C	3C	-----
Total	13	4	3	2	1

Another 2-4-2T was a latecomer to the area (Bushbury 3B)

6654	Chester	Longsight	3B	-----

A horizontal bar ----- indicates that it was withdrawn before this survey date.

6

The Freight Links

There were two freight links to cater for the varied and changing mineral and goods traffic in the area, including seasonal changes, especially in the transportation of coal which was the principal mineral commodity carried. Winter consumption, especially for household use and winter heating, created increased motive power demands which would then be followed by a summer decline. Nearby Bescot shed was also deeply involved in coal distribution from Cannock Chase and the other Midland area collieries. Special driving skills were needed to control long trains of non-fitted wagons downhill, preventing 'snatch' on the many gradients and descents caused by the geology of the area. Timing was not so vital as on the passenger services; steaming rates were lower (except for steep climbs) than those needed by sharply accelerating passenger trains. Braking of long, heavy coal trains was an acquired skill and a partnership with the guard in his van at the end of the train. This is a feature of freight operation no longer needed in an age of diesel-hauled, air-braked and custom-designed bulk carriers, which replaced the wooden planked, 13-ton 'minerals'.

Mainline Working – The 'Camdens', Locomotives and Men

The Walsall to Camden fully or partially fitted freight duty was, according to Ryecroft men, the oldest freight and largest operating link duty in the history of the shed. It is believed that it started just after the shed was opened in 1877 and was run by Ryecroft men until the shed closed for steam traction in 1957. The duty was shared by Camden Town shed, but Ryecroft worked the duty for long periods, Camden presumably being fully occupied with its commitment to long-distance passenger services. To Ryecroft men it was a coveted and honoured duty, such that drivers and firemen waited years for a vacancy to be available in this link. Crews were regularly known to spend between five and ten years on the duty. One had to be a fine engineman, a regular timekeeper and a loyal servant to the company to be even considered for the job. It was better paid being a double-trip lodging turn, with enginemen lodging in the metropolis.

The train ran during the years given above, with very little deviation from its allocated departure time, which dated back to the beginning of the service. It was one of a vast network of fast overnight freights to numerous London yards and docks introduced early in L&NWR days. Others originated from Holyhead, Carlisle, Liverpool, Manchester and Crewe. The Walsall Long Street (Bodleys) to Camden, calling at Bescot and Stechford, was timed to be the first arrival of these 'overnights' to London. The train was extremely important to Walsall manufacturers, craftsmen and tradesmen, enabling them to get their goods to London quickly on a regular timed basis. The town's leather manufactories made full use of its availability for many, many years.

The oldest recollections regarding the 'Camdens' were made available by retired Ryecroft driver Jack Reynolds, who spent forty-nine years at the depot. In interview, Jack Reynolds states that his father worked the train in the 1890s with the famous old Webb '18in goods', commonly known as 'Cauliflowers'. Jack continued the tradition of railway service by starting at Ryecroft in 1904. With details passed down by senior and younger Ryecroft drivers, a record of locomotive types and numbers associated with the service has been built up. The 'Cauliflowers' were used until about 1902, when, with loads getting heavier, Jack remembers the larger 2-8-0 four-cylinder compounds being assigned to the service. Fortunately, he has a photograph of one of shed 9's (Ryecroft) allocation for this service, No.2055, being prepared at the depot for the Camden job. The 2-8-0s worked on the service until around the end of the First World War. The trains were heavily loaded throughout the wartime years with vast quantities of leather goods such as harnesses and saddles for horses and mules, being Walsall's specialist contribution to the War Department. These goods were destined for animals serving in France. To help out with these heavy trains, Ryecroft began to use some of the Whale 'Experiment' Class 4-6-0s. From about 1922 onwards, the following 'Experiments' were allocated to Ryecroft: 1304 *Prometheus*; 2642 *Berenice*; 2625 *Buckland*; 2623 *Lord of the Isles*; 2621 *Ethelred*.

Firemen earned their pay on these engines on Camden turns. Their recollections are of 'Experiments' thrashing along the iron road in varying conditions – blinding snowstorms, heavy rain and gale-force winds. The class was renowned for heavy coal consumption and when the regulator was opened wide and the cut-off shortened, they could produce spectacular firework displays – coal going literally 'off the shovel and up the chimney'. A great sight to witness at night, but let's not forget the poor fireman. Former Ryecroft firemen recall these hard firing tasks with relish and good humour. In retirement they recognised that it was their job, but were pleased at the young firemen's lot being eased on more modern locomotives with their more efficient use of coal, especially the Stanier Class 5s. Further motive power arrived at shed 9 in about 1928, with some of the 'Prince of Wales' Class 4-6-0s to C.J. Bowen Cooke's design being allocated. His new 'Sir Gilbert Claughton' Class were taking over the mainline express trains, the larger engines relegating the 'Princes' (which had done some fifteen years of hard work on mainline duties between London and Carlisle), to smaller L&NWR (now LMS) sheds to handle freight and fast freight like the 'Camdens'. The prototype No.819 'Prince of Wales', but now remembered as LMS 5600, remained at Ryecroft until 1933, when it was scrapped.

Camdens loco 2745 about to leave Ryecroft shed 1936 with driver Billy Mills. (Jack Haddock Collection)

This had been the first superheated locomotive allocated to the depot, and, with its better steaming capacity, it was well suited to the Camden workings. Sister engine 5601 *Andromeda*, formerly L&NWR 1388, shared the Camden duties until 1933.

By 1933 the LMS was seriously reviewing its locomotive provision. With William Stanier becoming chief mechanical engineer, a locomotive revolution was imminent. In the two years between 1933 and 1935, the Camdens were mainly worked by well-used 'Claughtons' from Camden shed, their best locomotive obviously reserved for mainline express services. Subsequently, Camden (1B) often dumped some 'Claughtons' of indifferent quality on Ryecroft, which could obviously lead to poor timekeeping. To try to remedy this situation, the Ryecroft shedmaster ran trials with Midland Class 4F 0-6-0s, also extending the trials by using Fowler Horwich-designed 'Crab' 2-6-0s. The latter were obviously a much better provision, but some crews could not get them to steam; others, perhaps more open minded and flexible, getting very good results. The 0-6-0s in general put in a decent performance, but in the eyes of the ex-L&NWR men they were designed for mineral train work and their driving wheels were found to be too small for the long stretches of 40-50mph work needed between Stechford and London, especially for the up service. Despite this, the Midland Division Class 4s were working express freight trains over the more difficult road between Birmingham and London. Complaints of inadequate motive power were reaching headquarters at Crewe, and to Ryecroft's surprise in 1935, the depot was allocated two brand new Stanier 'Jubilee' Class 4-6-0 locomotives, Nos 5604 *Ceylon* and 5603 *Solomon Islands*.

The Stanier revolution took a little time to bear fruit. Early designs following Swindon low superheat traditions were proving a disappointment with poor steaming qualities and heavy coal consumption, a fact featuring in reports sent in from all depots operating 'Jubilees'. The problems were resolved by more adequate superheating, boiler tube revision, road-testing of modified examples and use of better coal. The two Ryecroft examples and Camden's provision for the balancing link were much improved, becoming very competent free-steaming units capable of running heavy, fast trains with better economy and efficient combustion. The pair became the flagship units at Ryecroft depot

Left: Ryecroft loco 5603 working Walsall to Camden Class 1 freight at Bescot, 1937. (Harry Russell)

Opposite: Seen from Ryecroft Junction signal box, the ex-LNWR Prince of Wales Class loco 5600 arrives on shed, *c.*1925. This type of loco also saw duty on the Walsall to Camdens. (Henry Green)

and were kept in a high state of cleanliness, well remembered as glistening and spotless in Midland maroon livery on the turntable in Mill Lane. One of these beauties, or any other named visitor appearing at the shed, would be a magnetic attraction for the many young trainspotters and adults passing the shed. For two years the 'dynamic duo' worked the Camdens plus many weekend seaside excursions, and very occasionally put in some service on local passenger and other more mundane duties.

In 1937 they were replaced by Nos 5595 *Southern Rhodesia* and 5651 *Shovell*, the standard joke of the time by Ryecroft firemen being that the latter was the most aptly named member of the class. In October of that year, following trials with two local Stanier-designed Class 5 4-6-0s (Nos 5038 and 5245), loaned to 3C for comparison with the 'Jubilees', a bonus came the fireman's way with the arrival of two brand new ex-works examples of the ubiquitous mixed traffic design. The 'Jubilees' were then transferred away to regular mainline express work. The newcomers, Nos 5417 and 5418, were an instant success and became most popular with the 'Camden' crews. The 6ft driving-wheel engines proved ideal for the service and proved the ultimate machine for the job, the up 'Camden' regularly being loaded to its maximum allowed fifty-five wagons.

After the outbreak of war, Nos 5417 and 5418 were transferred to Bescot in 1940, the pair continuing to work the express freight to London together with other Bescot Black '5s' (Nos 5322, 5387 and 5395), for most of the Second World War. Loads at this time would have been very heavy indeed. Ryecroft men were most fortunate during the London Blitz and flying-bomb era, thankfully being unaffected by such trauma. However, bomb damage could result in late running and diversions, with crews being on their footplates for anything up to eighteen or twenty hours.

In 1946 Ryecroft again received an allocation of Class 5s, these being Nos 4873, 5308, 5344 and 5395. Locomotive No.4873 was by unanimous consent the best engine ever to work from Ryecroft, an extremely free steamer and most economical on coal and water. This fine machine remained at Ryecroft until the depot closed for steam operations, and was then transferred to Bescot along with most of 3C's allocation. The well-liked No.4873 probably worked the 'Camdens' more times than any of its sisters, and was always a most welcome sight to the crews, when spotted on the front end of the train.

If the 5s were the 'first team' allocated to the 'Camdens', the 'second eleven' must receive a mention. Over the years and up to about 1948, Ryecroft 'Super D' 0-8-0s have been substituted on the 'Camdens', especially on a Friday night. The busy summer weekend excursions and seaside traffic made priority demands on the depots 4-6-0s. The Ds could do the job but, with their smaller wheels, good timekeeping was impossible. The prime objective was to get the train to London, and a punctual arrival on Saturday morning was not so critical, as forwarding of the merchandise was not so urgent. Being freight-pool workhorses, these locomotives did not receive the better quality coal always provided for the job, the Ds setting out with what was already in the tender, whatever its quality, plus of course a good topping up. For the locomotives allocated to the 'Camdens', a scheme was worked out for them to work a semi-fast local to Derby in the morning, enabling it to load grade 1 steam coal from Derby shed, before returning home to Ryecroft for servicing in readiness for the 8.45 p.m. departure to London. A balancing diagram for the engine for the overnight return service, arriving at Bodleys Yard at about 4.00 a.m., was to take a rake of empty coal wagons to Littleton Colliery sidings at Penkridge. The light engine return to Walsall enabled the locomotive to call in at Bushbury (Wolverhampton) to fill up with grade 1 fuel for another London visit, the refill at Camden before the return to Walsall being the grade 1 coal allocated to Camden's express passenger locomotives.

It was, however, in the interests of the railway company that Ryecroft's two express goods locomotives were kept to a strict diet of top-class coal. If Camden was desperately short of express locomotive power, a Ryecroft engine could be utilised. This led to Ryecroft engines being found as far away as Carlisle, Holyhead, Liverpool or Manchester; and inferior power substituted for the return trip to Walsall, where timing was not so important. After arriving at Camden Goods, the night up-Camden engine was relieved to work a parcels to Broad Street station in London, returning with a local passenger or empty stock working into Euston. It would then make its way to Camden shed for servicing, in readiness for the overnight return to Long Street (Bodleys) goods yard, Walsall.

For the up double trip, Ryecroft men booked on at 3C at 8.15 p.m., allowing thirty minutes for the 8.45 p.m. departure from Bodleys. The engine, previously prepared by

Ryecroft's own 45344 on shed prior to working a Canadian trade mission special to Carlisle, 1955. This was another type of Ryecroft loco to see duty on the Walsall to Camden freight. (Jack Haddock Collection)

Ryecroft, would be at Long Street already on its train awaiting departure. It would have been oiled round, steam pressure approaching blowing-off, brakes tested and raring to go. At precisely a couple of minutes before 8.45 p.m., shunting at Bodleys temporarily ceased to allow an on-time Camden departure. Bescot Brook sidings were the first (and nearby) call, to attach more wagons already assembled to join the train. By or before 9.25 p.m., Bescot was left behind for the train's next call at Stechford. The shunt to attach a further rake of prepared wagons was tightly time-limited to enable a 10.00 p.m. departure, allowing the double trip to precede the 10.05 p.m. all stations to Rugby. This would ensure a long succession of green signals all the way to Camden, which would be reached just after midnight. To follow the local would be catastrophic and result in many hold-ups after Rugby as the Camden's path would be lost. This could mean disastrous diversions via Northampton and up to two or three hours of extra duty for the crews, and faith broken with shippers with guarantees for on-time deliveries to the capital.

On arrival at Camden Town goods yard the crew were relieved by Camden men, the Ryecroft crew retiring to Camden shed to book off, wash, eat in the railwaymen's mess and retire to the hostel (barracks) for sleep. Most would sleep to mid-morning or later, the 3C men then being free for the afternoon to go sightseeing in London, attend a matinée at West End theatres or visit Kew Gardens, the latter being popular as many railwaymen were keen gardeners. If a lazy afternoon was envisaged it was time for a glass of ale at the Lansdown pub, situated just outside Camden shed, before it closed for the afternoon at about 2.00 p.m. This would then be followed by another nap or local 'mooch around' before the evening departure preparation in readiness for the long trip home. During the 1920–40 period of Depression, not many working men could afford a trip to London. It was only through careful saving throughout the year that a family could undertake a week's annual holiday at Blackpool or some other coastal resort. Day trips to London or elsewhere were usually out of the question, so being elevated to the 'Camdens' was highly sought after and considered a perk at company expense. The Saturday Camden arrival was always popular with the football-minded crews who were able to see an away match if Aston Villa, Wolves, West Bromwich Albion, Walsall or Birmingham were in town.

The return 'Camden' was not classed as an express service, being regarded more as a semi-fast freight with more interchange and pick-up points, so speed was not such a priority with this train. Booking on time at Camden was 7.40 p.m. for the locomotive which proceeded to Camden goods for its 8 p.m. departure. From Camden it worked via the slow lines to Northampton to pick up and put down vans; here the train loco did its own shunting. Next port of call was Rugby where more wagons were detached or collected; again the shunting was handled by the Ryecroft men. At both of these main yards, time was often lost because of the density of overnight freight workings, timed to run after the cessation of most passenger trains, which at all times had priority of road over freight traffic. Such goods traffic increased dramatically after about 11.30 p.m., with the return 'Camden' allocated a slot north from Rugby at about 12.30 a.m. A clear run could usually be expected as the Coventry/Birmingham line was accessed just north of the busy Rugby yards. The locomotive could then be opened up for an uninterrupted series of green signals to Stechford for more pick-up/set-down activity. Arrival at Bescot was mainly to drop-off most of the train, which would then be split for forwarding to various Black Country towns and works. The locomotive and crew then made a steady trundle to Long Street, Walsall, and ultimately bed.

Ken Horan never worked on the 'Camdens' in his firing days, but recalls that he and his driver (Eddie Hughes) had sometimes been hanging about at Ryecroft in the Special Link and had nothing to do all night. As there was no cafeteria facilities at Ryecroft, they were never able to get a hot meal but occasionally they were sent to 'relieve' the crew coming in from Camden at Stechford, presumably to break up the boredom or get them out of sight. Whatever the reason it was no advantage to the 'booked' crew who either came back on the footplate or retired to the brake van at the rear of the train. Our two worldly-wise, however, on arrival at Bescot and dropping off the bulk of the train, were determined to make the best of Bescot's hot-meal facilities. Ringing up the 'bobby' (signalman) they would inform him they would not be ready for half an hour. The guard, regular crew and reliefs piled into the Bescot 'Ritz' for a piping hot breakfast of bacon, sausage, egg, beans and fried bread, with tea or coffee, all of which post-war could be purchased for 1*s*. With the temporary 'locomotive fault' rectified, it was all aboard to tow the few remaining vans to Long Street. It was never considered as 'milking' the system, just a case of what's good enough for Bescot is good enough for Ryecroft! Although 3C could be considered as a sub-shed of upstart Bescot, its men would never allow any suspicion of it being inferior!

7

The Shunting Link

This link provided the manpower to operate the locomotives, in various strategic yards and sidings. Their duties were to break and remake formations of mineral and freight wagons, for onward delivery to both local and long-distance destinations. This link could be considered as a training ground for newly qualified drivers and firemen, but the impression this gives would be a gross over-simplification. It was a responsible, skilled and extremely important job. In steam days and even to this day, wagons were sorted in a complex arrangement of sidings, to be reformed according to destination. It was a job where safety, common sense and an acquired skill was used over sustained periods of time, punctuated with shorter periods of rest and inactivity. It was always carried out in a state of co-operation with the busy shunter on foot, who would be releasing couplings with a long hooked pole as the shunt was in motion. Careful co-operation could make a shunter's lot easy; a coupling under tension would be almost impossible to move. The shunter's skill was to select the vital moment to flick off the coupling whilst maintaining balance and inertia, moving along the wagons during the operation. With vehicles being released and finding their own way through pre-set points, the dangers faced by constantly moving shunters on foot are obvious. Shunters' commands were often answered, and reversal movements preceded, by coded whistles from the foot plate in the constant stop/go activity – by day and night. Some vital long-distance trains (e.g. the 'Camdens') had to be completed to leave at their booked time otherwise vital slots might be lost, thereby causing delay to critical arrival times of valuable and urgently needed goods. The sonorous clank of buffer on buffer, the shouted instructions, the urgent acceleration followed by controlled braking backed by staccato exhaust, wheel flange squeal and the hiss of steam as safety valves popping all combined to create the 'symphony' of the yard, so typical of the past but not heard today.

The shunting link often used elderly motive power for their operations – vintage locomotives solidly built, economic and once considered mainline freight power. In shunting, their services still proved admirable and dependable, in a job where relatively low power outputs were necessary. This was the realm of the elderly Midland and L&NWR

class 2 0-6-0 freight engine, often sixty to seventy years old and rebuilt several times. They were true veterans, but still capable and efficient machines. The shunting link serviced the following shunts: the Birchills shunt, the Norton Canes hump shunt, Leighswood (Pelsall), Essington interchange, Midland Yard shunt, Bridgeman Place and Long Street (Bodleys) shunt. Other small yards were shunted by the locomotives operating pick-up goods services (e.g. The Stafford double trip) and additional shunts operated according to traffic requirements. At Norton Junction, a flat shunt rectified any hump-shunting mistakes, and attached and detached wagons to and from passing freight trains. Brewers shunt dealt with timber for Brooks & Ortons timber yard, Hales timber yard, Nevilles Foundry and the Oak Tanning Co. This shunt was additional to, and worked by, the Bridgeman Place locomotive. Brewers was a very complicated shunt between Ryecroft junction and Walsall, access being situated halfway between those points. Trains for these customers were made up on Ryecroft shed with the engine in the middle of its train. The Ryecroft signal man had the problem of moving the shunt across the up and down mainlines within his very tight operating margins. The shunt driver, often a passed fireman gaining experience, was also highly unpopular with the disposal staff on the shed, whose routines were seriously affected as the train was made up.

Norton Junction Shunt

Ryecroft Shed Shunting Duties. The Norton Junction sidings shunt, Ryders Hayes, Pelsall and coal traffic from Cannock Chase Collieries

In this section I will record information on Norton Junction sidings, and the workings to them from the Cannock Chase coalfields. I will commence with the known history of the original sidings in early L&NWR days, linked with information given by retired Ryecroft and Bescot drivers covering the period from about 1905 until its closure to coal traffic in 1964. I shall also include the methods and system of filtering all coal for local and long-distance areas of England for which Norton Junction was the main sorting sidings.

The first sidings at Ryders Hayes consisted of five lines running parallel to the Walsall to Lichfield line situated on the Pelsall side of the tracks. Near Ryders Hayes level crossing was a signal box controlling the sidings. It would appear that the first function of the sidings was to accommodate the coal traffic from the various Pelsall collieries and goods from the large Pelsall ironworks. The description of the lines will commence with the workings on the Pelsall side of Ryders Hayes, and follow with the expansion of Norton Junction, from the opening of the Cannock extension branch on 25 April 1879. Following the line with the aid of a map dated 1884 it would appear that the Pelsall collieries were at their peak period. The line from Ryders Hayes ran parallel with the present Ryders Hayes Lane. A level crossing was situated on the Norton Road and the crossing keeper's house still stands today as 60, Norton Road, Pelsall. The line ran across Pelsall top common to serve Pelsall collieries 8 and 9. A present-day location for these pits is the site of School Lane and Wolverhampton Road, opposite the 'Swan' Inn. Sidings for No.8 were situated around the pit which, according to local people, possessed a shunting engine. The line from collieries 8 and 9 then crossed the Wolverhampton Road at the site of the present-day Highfield Road, continuing through Pelsall Wood and over the Wyrley & Essington Canal to run directly into the huge ironworks with its extensive sidings. From the ironworks the line ran parallel with the canal to another colliery called the Ebenesar pit, known to Pelsall locals as the Plant pit. Its most famous happening was in 1905 when a miner named Benny Davies descended the pit for duty and promptly disappeared never to be seen again. At this pit the branch line from Ryders Hayes terminated. Another line ran from the Pelsall village side of the ironworks to link up with Pelsall No.10 Colliery, situated almost in Fishley Village or Little Bloxwich. En route to the pit, the line crossed Wood Lane which actually possessed a signal box with gates. Local senior citizens talk of stories handed down to them from their parents about the amount of horse-drawn traffic to and from the ironworks, presumably the ponies and traps of the management commuting to work. It is assumed that the gentry, maintaining their usual rights and privileges, had the level crossing built for them to ensure their safety.

The activity in the Pelsall ironworks and collieries must have been at its zenith in about 1870, and one can imagine the noise of the works, the pits and the engines shunting the sidings. This activity came to an end by about 1890 with the closure of the ironworks, made certain by competition from German and other European manufacturers, forcing them out of business. At around the same time the pits were closing as they became worked out, and also due to the newer Cannock Chase pits being opened to produce better grade coal. By about 1900, this railway network to Ryders Hayes came to a standstill.

I can find no record of Ryecroft L&NWR engines ever using these sidings. It seems that the ironworks and colliery shunters bought their loads to the three long sidings situated along where the present-day Ryders Hayes Lane is sited. The L&NWR engines then pulled the trains to their own sidings. On 25 April 1879 a line opened from Norton Junction to Hednesford to facilitate movements of coal from the numerous collieries in the Cannock Chase area. This line branched off the L&NWR main Walsall to Lichfield line at the Brownhills side of Ryders Hayes sidings, towards Norton Canes. At first this was just a double-track line to Norton, then single to Hednesford. All coal trains from the Chase came down to be sorted in the sidings running parallel to the mainline, but with coal traffic getting heavier, more sidings had to be constructed. Gradually new sidings were put in alongside the line to Norton and Hednesford, starting at the Brownbills end of the parallel sidings to the main Brownhills to Wolverhampton Road. At this time the narrow bridge must have been built to span the line, today known as the Pelsall Highbridges. Gradually the sidings grew to what is now known as Norton Junction.

15 August 1881 saw the opening of a line from the Littleworth extension railway on to the L&NWR Norton branch, whilst on 13 January 1894 a line from the Coppice Colliery at Heath Hayes was opened to bring coal to Norton Green Colliery on the Norton branch. This colliery was always referred to by railwaymen as the Five Ways Colliery and to the local residents as the Fair Lady. During the period from 1880 to 1900, Norton Junction gradually evolved into a major sorting and distributing marshalling yard to supply coal to the Midlands conurbation and also to the London area plus other long-distance destinations.

Norton Junction hump shunt staff with 'Super D' 49241, 1949. (Jack Haddock Collection)

The following facts have emerged during tape-recorded conversations with retired Ryecroft railwaymen about Norton Junction in latter L&NWR days, the LMS era and finally BR days, concerning the Ryecroft and Bescot train movements from the various collieries. Obviously there had to be a regular routine of harnessing all the coal traffic. The system that evolved in L&NWR days at Norton Junction survived more or less until the yard closed to coal traffic in 1964. Ryecroft Shed provided a shunting engine on a twenty-four-hour shunt from the 1879 opening of the sidings until it closed for steam engines in 1957. Just after nationalisation in 1948, Ryecroft took delivery of a new diesel shunter especially for Norton Junction hump shunt. This shunt, according to Ryecroft drivers, was the second hardest job in the London Midland region, being second only to Toton. Diesel number 3021 was designed with a double-reduction drive system to help cope with heavy loads. It was accepted very favourably with drivers and thus secured the working until final closure of coal trains at Norton Junction. The duty carried on even after Ryecroft Shed had changed to diesel multiple-unit workings in 1958. The shunting engine spent most of its time on the Highbridges side of the marshalling yard where a shunting hump was provided. By the shunting hump was a small L&NWR type signal box, water tower and large shunters cabin. Here resided the head shunter who virtually controlled this large area of sidings. Arriving trains could vary in size from twenty wagons hauled by a Webb coal engine, to a train consisting of fifty-five wagons with a L&NWR Class D or 'Super D' in charge. The method of dealing with coal trains arriving from one of the Chase pits was as follows. On the approach to the sidings just before the canal bridge were two notice boards, the first of which was 'Stop', positioned just prior to some facing points. The second notice board was near the hump with enough distance to accommodate the maximum fifty-five wagon train, and read, 'All trains must wait for instructions from the head shunter'. He was responsible for meeting each train. The procedure was to ensure that the brakes of the wagon were pinned down as the stop board was situated on a down gradient. The train engine was then permitted to run down to the Ryders Hayes end of the sidings. This locomotive then backed onto a ready made-up train of coal for a certain destination, usually departing in the path of a local passenger train towards Walsall. Meanwhile, the original train now standing uncoupled in the siding had to be sorted. The hump-shunting engine ran to the rear of the train and started to split up the train by pushing wagons over the hump. The big problem here was that, prior to the Second World War, a lot of wagons were privately owned. This entailed a lot of skilful manoeuvring to make up a train for a particular district, the idea being to enable trains dropping off wagons at company's private sidings on a main passenger line to do so with the minimum of shunting so as not to interfere with the working passenger time-table.

The hump-shunting engine from Ryecroft Shed was for many years always an L&NWR Super D. It shunted twenty-four hours a day, leaving Ryecroft Shed early on Monday morning to work through the week until Saturday lunch time. When its coal supply ran out it was substituted with a fresh engine, and a new shift crew took over. The crews worked a three-shift system of approximately eight hours. An extract from a Ryecroft driver's log book with which I was presented concerns a driver Mr Horace Smith of Essex Street, Walsall, and reads, 'Duty for the 7th October 1935 - Norton Junction hump shunt, engine number 9283 - 11.30 a.m. to 7.25 p.m'.

These shunting engines were usually the ones which were about to receive heavy shopping and overhaul at Crewe works. When received back from the works, the Super Ds then proceeded to work heavy coal trains. These locomotives did, in fact, work coal trains of some fifty-five loose coupled wagons to Willesden Junction in London. This regular duty of some five trains per day was allocated to Bescot shed before the Second World War, but in wintertime several special trains ran with Ryecroft Super Ds. During the winter the shunting engine was working virtually non-stop, crews being allowed only one twenty-minute meal break. To assist during periods of heavy traffic, Ryecroft shed allocated another shunting engine to Norton Junction. This engine always worked from the bottom part of the yard near the old sidings known as the flat shunt. It had fairly regular hours of work, starting duty at Ryecroft Shed at approximately 8.30 a.m. and arriving back on shed at 5.30 p.m. In another extract from Driver H. Smith's log we find the entry, 'Norton Junction flat shunt 18th June 1936, engine number 22907, 11.11 a.m. to 7.15 p.m'. A Class 2 Midland engine or an L&NWR coal tank was the usual engine allocated this job. A regular working for the flat shunt engine was to make a few trips during the day over the mainline to two sidings near the L&NWR Ryders Hayes signal box. From these sidings ran a branch line to Walsall Wood Colliery whose engines brought their loaded coal trains up to the sidings and picked up empty wagons for the colliery. Here, the colliery engine and the flat shunt engine just exchanged loads. However, prior to 2 January 1909 the L&NWR engines always worked through to Walsall Wood. Empty coal trains to Norton Junction arrived in the sidings on the Pelsall village side of the yard. A shunting hump was provided for the empties, and the train engine was partly responsible for shunting its own train. During the 1920s and 1930s these empty trains used to arrive at intervals, day and night during the winter months. The trains, usually comprising about fify-five wagons, were more or less sorted for the various pits.

Norton Junction sidings showing signal box No.2 which was used to control the hump, 1966. (Jack Haddock Collection)

After this duty the locomotive usually retired to the bottom of the loaded wagons end of the yard to work another train, or ran light engine to one of the Cannock or Hednesford pits to bring back more coal to be sorted at Norton Junction.

Another Ryecroft duty for these sidings, usually a Webb coal engine, which started from Ryecroft shed at about 6.30 a.m. and worked through until the job was finished, was to help out on the empty wagon hump. It's main task was to distribute empty wagons to all the surrounding collieries. Being only a Class 2F engine, it used to take about thirty wagons on each journey, but ex-driver Fred Haywood tells of a time-saving fiddle. The engine crew and guard conspired to take two trains at once, namely sixty wagons, and the main problem was to ascend the heavy gradient out of the yard. To do this the fireman would operate the sanding gear as far as the canal bridge to the top of the gradient of about 400 yards. The old Webb coal engine with regulator fully open would make a charge for the bank. Anyone who has seen one of these engines performing one of these feats will remember the firework display of red-hot cinders and smoke box char being thrown 50ft or more into the air. The engine usually made it up the gradient but, on occasions, the Super D of the hump shunt had to come to the rescue.

So far the facts have been concerned with the locomotives of Ryecroft shed and their duties at Norton Junction, but turning to the administration of the yard, the following information has been obtained.

The man in charge of Norton Junction sidings was the Pelsall stationmaster. It was always the practice on the L&NWR and later the LMS system, for the stationmaster to be responsible for the running of the local goods yard. For a village like Pelsall it must have been a record for so large a shunting complex to be situated adjacent to a small village station. He lived at the station in a company house and was in control of some thirty staff. They consisted of a yard foreman and two head shunters of Norton Junction Yard, who in turn had three shunters working the three-shift hump shunt. To assist the shunters were two other shunters, sometimes known as runners, whose job it was to run with the moving wagons to pin down the brakes if the wagons were going too fast, then to couple the wagons to make up a ready-made train. This was quite a dangerous job. This was the job where the small L&NWR signal box had its use. All the points radiating from the hump were controlled from this box and the routine was for the head shunter to place a chalk mark number of the siding on the truck leaving the hump for the signalman to spot, and then proceed to move the appropriate levers to allocate the wagon to the correct siding. Problems sometime arose because some wagons were fast runners whilst others were slower. The reason for this was that many of the older wagons had grease-filled axle boxes, whilst the newer wagons ran on oil baths. Railwaymen always referred to the grease-filled wagons as 'gammys'. One can appreciate the signalman's predicament having a slow wagon almost on the facing points and a fast wagon approaching. It must have been quite an art for the signalman and needed a good understanding with the hump shunter uncoupling the wagons. Mishaps did occur at times, but with the aid of special rerailing blocks supplied for such emergencies and some skilful control by the engine driver, wagons were soon back on the road. Some, however, had to be withdrawn to the crippled wagon sidings where three men were employed as wagon examiners, working the three-shift system, whose job it was to examine every wagon passing through the junction and to carry out minor running repairs where necessary. To deal with major repairs a regular pick-up freight train from Norton sidings ran via Bescot to Vauxhall and Duddeston, taking the crippled wagons to the main repair depot. This train ran during slack periods between passenger trains and travelled at a very slow speed.

Mention should be made of the permanent way staff who maintained the track in the yard and also the track from the various collieries. They had their own cabin in the yard and worked the three-shift system. For extra help on yard duties in times of heavy traffic or in sickness, Bescot supplied the necessary staff.

The lighting system employed in the yard was gas lamps, which, by today's standards of marshalling yard lighting, was very primitive.

One time of the year when Norton Junction came to a rest was the August Bank Holiday period, when rows of passenger coaches stored alongside the coal wagons could be seen. This was to ease the pressure on congested Walsall sidings. It was common during the years prior to the 1923 railway grouping for some thirty to forty special trains to leave Walsall for the North Wales resorts and Blackpool at holiday times. It was the practice for Ryecroft engines to run light up to Norton Junction to pick up the coaches and then run into Walsall station to load with passengers. Trains left Walsall at approximately ten-minute intervals by the flat and easy route via Bushbury to the various resorts. After the holiday the yard gradually came back to life.

Having recorded the workings of the Ryecroft engine crews from Norton Junction, we now turn to the working of coal traffic from the various Cannock Chase pits.

Norton Junction hump shunt staff with D Class loco, *c.*1922. (Jack Haddock Collection)

Coal Train Workings from Cannock Chase Pits to Norton Junction

The normal routine for traffic from Cannock Chase collieries in L&NWR and LMS days was to filter each train load of coal across the Norton branch. Trains from the Hednesford pits left the Walsall to Rugeley line at East Cannock Junction. It should be explained at this point, that some of the information in these notes was obtained from railwaymen who worked over these lines, but certain assumptions have been made based upon notes contained in *A Chronology of the Railways of the West Midlands 1808-1954* published by the Stephenson Locomotive Society. From this publication we learn that the line from Walsall to Cannock and Norton branch was opened on 1 February 1858. It would appear that the branch line must have been the first line from East Cannock Junction as we know it today, to Norton near the site of the Norton Green Colliery. Here the level crossing was situated on the Walsall to Heath Hayes Road. Several citizens of Norton have given accounts of a wooden platform on the Cannock side of the crossing, leaving us to wonder whether there was ever a passenger service over this section, even if it was only used by workmens' trains. More possible is the use of the line by coal trains only, taking coal to Cannock for onward distribution, as this section of route was opened on 7 November 1859. It was not until 25 April 1879 that the line was opened throughout to Hednesford.

We now have the accounts of various Ryecroft locomotive drivers of the working of the line from Norton Junction to the furthermost colliery situated at Brereton.

Starting up the bank out of Norton Junction, the first sidings on the left were Harrison's sidings. Ryecroft engines only worked into these sidings; the colliery engines brought up the coal from Harrison's pit in Lime Lane, Pelsall, to the main sidings. This pit was known locally as the 'Grove' pit. One can remember the sight from the top of a Walsall Corporation double-decker bus of the hump-backed level crossing in Lime Lane. From the top of the bus, as the colliery shunter passed over the crossing it would be level with one's viewpoint. On this crossing in 1957 an accident occurred when a heavily laden tarmac lorry collided with one of the colliery shunters. Fortunately, no one was hurt in the accident. The sidings were in operation until the closure of the Norton branch in 1964.

The next sidings along the line served Conduit Colliery, Norton. Some of the sidings ran parallel to the mainline with points at each end, so that by using these points the Ryecroft engines would reverse the empty wagons into Conduit and then pull away the loaded ones. Near these sidings were the remains of other tracks leading to a colliery long since disused known as the Wilkin Colliery. No Ryecroft men I spoke to can ever remember hauling trains from this pit. Located between the Conduit Colliery and the next colliery, the Norton Green Colliery was the road level crossing with small signal box and signals. It was perhaps a blessing that road traffic in the 1920s and 1930s was fairly light as there was a regular procession of coal trains. Ryecroft driver Fred Haywood recalls an incident on the crossing in 1934 when, during a cold weather spell in January he was the fireman on a 'Super D' No.9375 and was working a train from one of the Hednesford pits. This train of some twenty wagons was on a regular weekly duty. On the first Monday of this duty a build up of coal wagons at Norton Junction stopped the train at Conduit Colliery. Orders were then received to shunt off its train into the Conduit sidings, then return to Ryecroft Shed light engine, but owing to the Conduit sidings being full they were instructed to back the wagons into the Norton Green sidings just over the level crossing, with orders to pick up again on one of the following weekdays whilst working the same duty. It was not until the following Friday that the same crew, again with 'Super D' 9375, left Hednesford with its allocation of twenty wagons. It had been a very cold week with ice and snow with temperatures mainly below zero. The orders were to pick up Monday's wagons and take the two trains of forty wagons down to Norton Junction. The procedure was to reverse into the Norton Green sidings, couple up to Monday's wagons, whistle for the crossing gates to open and then start for Norton Junction.

However, the train got halfway over the crossing when it came to a full stop. The 'Super D' had a full head of steam and was in good condition; it was soon discovered that the problem was caused by frozen axle-boxes on the wagons which had been standing since the previous week. It took about half an hour to get the icebound trucks back into the sidings and to clear the crossing. Fred Haywood well remembers the Walsall to Hednesford bus waiting at the crossing and instead of the usual wave from the bus driver he remembers a clenched fist. This was just one small problem of the Norton Junction and Cannock Chase railway complex and it serves to illustrate the additional hazards of the hard-working life of pre-war days.

Another interesting snippet of information refers to the single line running from Conduit Colliery to the Five Ways Colliery at Heath Hayes. This pit was also known as the 'Coppice Colliery', or to the local residents as the 'Fair Lady'. The Ryecroft men had a duty here which was normally handled by a Webb coal engine. To get to the Five Ways one started downhill to pass under the main road to Heath Hayes, then up a severe gradient of about one mile to Five Ways. Under the bridge between the two gradients there was no drainage system, although in L&NWR and early LMS days a motor pump had been installed to pump water clear. At certain times during heavy rain the bridge would flood to firebox level and several Ryecroft men tell of rushing through the flood water at speed and getting soaked to the skin in the process. The pump was supposed to keep the bridge hole clear of water, and Frank Rigby, who was a fitter at Ryecroft in the 1930s, can recall being called out to start the pump at every good downfall of rain. To put a stop to the unsatisfactory arrangement, the LMS installed a modern electric pump in the late 1930s which was set to cut in automatically when just a few inches of water were lying under the bridge.

For many years the coal engines slogged between Conduit and Five Ways. This line was worked with a staff or tablet supplied from the Conduit sidings signal box and usually the Ryecroft engines only worked this line during daytime. At certain times, owing to a shortage of railway staff on engines during the winter peak periods of coal output, the Five Ways Colliery shunter was allowed to bring coal down to the Conduit sidings. This was achieved by one of the colliery officials coming down to Conduit signal box to collect the tablet and also the keys for unlocking the facing points at the top of the severe gradient running into Five Ways siding. I am told that this working often occurred during the night in wintertime due to Five Ways sidings becoming full with loaded wagons as a result of twenty-four-hour working at the pit, and the only alternative was to use the colliery engines to help out the LMS engines. This part of Norton Canes around Norton Green and Conduit collieries was a constant hub of activity with Ryecroft engines and crews, although Bescot locomotives and men also shared duties at times.

The line between Norton Green and Norton Junction was about two and half miles long and of double track. The up line to Norton Junction was allowed by the L&NWR (and later LMS) control, to operate on the permissive block basis. This enabled coal trains to draw up and wait behind each other to await their turn at the Norton Junction hump shunt. Many Ryecroft men recall a queue of as many as ten trains waiting during severe winter weather, or line blockage at Norton Junction sidings. Fred Haywood recalled another winter duty on this line. He was fireman on 'Super D' No.9173 during the winter of 1934 and his train was positioned in a line of coal trains when, after about ten hours of duty, he was relieved by a fresh crew. Upon returning to duty next day, some eighteen hours later, he and his driver actually relieved a crew back on No.9173 which was still standing in the same section that it had been when he left it previously. One should bear in mind that these engine crews often had to walk from Norton Junction in darkness and in all weathers to find their trains. The firemen also had to ensure that the engine had a tank full of water before entering one of the queues. There are no recorded instances or railwaymen's memories of any of these engines ever running short of coal and water during these delays, thanks to the foresight of the locomotive men.

If coal supplies were held up for any length of time at Five Ways or Conduit collieries, it could be transported over the Midland Railways sidings running into both collieries.

Norton Junction sidings showing No.1 box when the sidings were known as Bescot North surplus wagon sidings, 1966. (Jack Haddock Collection)

Colliery engines performed this duty by taking them as far as Norton Pool sidings, near Brownhills. The Midland Railway then ran the coal down to Aldridge. Following the 1923 grouping of the railways, the Ryecroft men began to work these trains also. The double-track line from Norton Canes was known as the Cannock Extension Railway, but to Ryecroft men it was always the Norton Branch.

From the Norton Green sidings the line ran to East Cannock Junction as single track worked by the staff or tablet system. The Leacroft Colliery ran its coal onto this line and supplied about three trains each day.

With the vast amount of coal to be moved to Norton Junction, it was collected in the large Hednesford Town sidings from the following collieries: Mid Cannock, East Cannock, West Cannock, Cannock Wood, Wimblebury, Hednesford No.1 and Brereton. Here at Hednesford was another regular shunting engine working a twenty-four-hour duty. It was always a 'Super D' for dealing with heavy trains. It was a residential shunt duty with three regular crews who alone worked this job in L&NWR days. In later years the duty came under Bescot Shed, although at times both sheds supplied engines for short periods. This was a very busy shunt dealing with hundreds of wagons each day. Most empty wagon trains came up the Walsall to Cannock Line, to Hednesford sidings, to immediately take up a coal train to join the queue to Norton junction. A well-remembered Ryecroft duty was to bring a loaded train from Brereton Colliery which meant a hard slog for the 'Super D' up the gradient from Rugeley to Hednesford. Occasionally the Hednesford shunt engine had to come to the rescue as a banker. In the First World War a military railway was constructed across Cannock Chase starting from the Hednesford Sidings to the L&NWR

line at Milford, although there was never a physical connection between the two systems. One Ryecroft man, Jim Abbotts, can remember working on this line.

The Hednesford residential drivers had some knowledge of the colliery lines running into Hednesford sidings. At certain times they have worked the Walsall District Engineers Saloon coach to some of these pits. It is believed that these visits by the engineer were to assess proposals for LMS engines to assist colliery engines in an emergency. The engineer's staff also helped the colliers with track maintenance. It is a well-known fact that many railway staff, gangers and platelayers found employment with the collieries upon retirement from the Railway Co.

Ryecroft and Bescot sheds supplied men and engines to filter all this traffic from Cannock, Hednesford and Norton pits from Victorian times right up to 1964. The 'Super Ds' and coal engines of the L&NWR did yeoman service for many years. After the 1923 grouping Midland 0-6-0 tender engines of Johnson Class 2, 3, and 4 also put in many years service. After the Second World War the Stanier Class 5 and Class 8 locomotives worked the line until closure. On one notable occasion in 1964, just prior to the complete closure of the Norton Junction to East Cannock section, a special passenger train ran over the branch. The promoter of this special train was the Midland area branch of the Stephenson Locomotive Society. The train consisted of eight coaches hauled by one of the then four surviving 'Super Ds', No.49361 of Bescot Shed. Shortly after came complete closure of the colliery system between Norton Junction and the Cannock to Rugeley line.

British Railways renamed Norton Junction as 'Bescot North Empty Wagon' sidings, its only use in 1976 being to store steel wagons during a recession in the steel industry, along with ballast wagons awaiting weekend maintenance duties. At one time an oil company wanted to develop the sidings into a vast oil distribution centre for motor transport, but local Pelsall residents opposed the possibility of a potential fire risk right on the doorstep of the village. In the meantime, coal, in the form of pulverised slack, continued to pass through Norton Junction on the 'merry-go-round' trains from the Nottinghamshire coalfields to the Midland power stations. One wonders what the old-time shunters would think of these trains that never need to be uncoupled or shunted by hand. Perhaps they might think that they were born too soon.

Looking back at the operation and working of Norton Junction as I tape-recorded the memories of drivers and firemen of Ryecroft Shed, I now realise how important this junction was in its heyday to commerce, trade and industry and for household coal supplies. Cannock Chase coal was often carried far afield, judging by the experience of ex-miner Cliff Harvey, who was born and bred in Heath Hayes, within a few hundred yards of the Coppice Colliery. He tells of the time as a young lad spending his school holidays with a relative in Birkenhead. One day he went out with his uncle complete with wheelbarrow to procure the household coal supply. To his surprise, when entering the local coal yard, he saw among the wagons several bearing the name 'Coppice Colliery'.

Norton Junction was always alive, and residents of Pelsall can still recall the noise of the buffers of trucks hitting each other after the run down the hump. The noise was very noticeable when the wind was in the east, and added to the noise of the wagons was the usual chorus of engine whistles. What a place to work in the winter during the fog and in

Norton Junction sidings taken from inside signal box No.1, 1966. (Jack Haddock Collection)

the snow. The only solace the men had were the many small cabins with the roaring fires blazing, and the wet coats drying out. Fortunately they were never short of coal!

Standing head and shoulders above the sidings was the large L&NWR signal box from which vantage point one had a view of the whole yard. One wonders about the problems men faced and the decisions that had to be made from the signal box, such as shunting across the mainline, or to decide how many coal trains to fit in between the passenger trains. Also remember that someone was always in residence in this box for over 100 years. With that thought I conclude these stories gathered from ex-Ryecroft and Bescot Shed staff who have so kindly allowed them to be tape-recorded and have thus ensured the preservation of some local railway history which might otherwise have been completely forgotten.

The Leighswood Branch Shunt – a Ryecroft and Bescot Combined Shunting Duty

On 14 November 1878 the L&NWR opened a branch line from the main Walsall to Lichfield line to serve the Leighswood Colliery, Aldridge. From Leighswood Junction some quarter of a mile south of Pelsall Station, the line passed through pleasant countryside on a downhill gradient, before passing beneath the Walsall to Lichfield road in Shelfield, some 40 yards from the Spring Cottage public house. The line continued downhill from Shelfield to where it crossed Stubbers Green Road. There was then quite a steep gradient to the colliery, and it reached its apex on crossing the canal. By the canal the line was afflicted by a series of twists and curves which required guard rails to prevent

The Leighswood shunt showing loco 58157 at the Atlas works siding on 8 September 1953. (F.W. Shuttleworth)

derailments. On the Aldridge side of the canal near to the colliery was the Victoria brick and tile works, with a siding running from Leighswood Colliery to the brickworks. It is thought both concerns were in the same management and ownership in those days. Just off Stubbers Green Village was another small colliery, the Stubbers Green Colliery, and another brickworks taking its name from the village, both concerns linked to the railway. From 1878 until 1 April 1880 the colliery engine was responsible for bringing the Stubbers Green Colliery output to Leighswood Junction, and from the latter date, L&NWR locomotives shared the duty. With the L&NWR taking complete control of the line and its traction from 14 June 1880, the colliery locomotive was then restricted to making up trains within the pit's confines.

Train weights and lengths were increasing at this time, with the tile works finding the railway more suited to its needs than the canal. This meant the L&NWR had to provide more powerful locomotives to handle the tonnage. Prior to 1908 no knowledge of the branch's working can be ascertained, but information from Ryecroft and Bescot drivers confirms that just before the First World War, Ryecroft always worked a daytime shunt from about 7 a.m. to 4.30 p.m. This culminated in a trainload, mainly of tiles, being taken to Bridgeman Place Yard, Walsall. Bescot men then worked from about 5.30 p.m.until midnight, but had to deliver their coal trains to Wednesbury Town station's centre line, the procedure then being to push the train up to the Great Western sidings for destinations on their system. Bescot also often had to work a special train loaded with high-density blue constructional bricks to the GWR. The first locomotives to use the Leighswood Branch after the North Western took control were Webb 0-6-0 saddle-tanks with no cab and hand brakes only. Some were later fitted with small cabs, but at no time were they considered powerful or comfortable enough by their crews. Nevertheless, crews must have performed miracles with these small locomotives of limited tractive effort. These engines

The Leighswood shunt, again with loco 58157 on 8 September 1953. (F.W. Shuttleworth)

were in evidence until about 1910, but with heavier loads and more trips needed, motive power was upgraded by an allocation of extra Webb 0-6-0 17in coal engines, one of which was allocated to the Leighswood shunt. Ryecroft then had nine or ten and Bescot about fifteen of the type. Occasionally the coal tank version (nicknamed a 'Gadget') was substituted for the job, but it was mainly a 17in goods job until just after the Second World War.

The tortuous twisting gradients of the branch often induced cases of locked buffers between engine and tender. This resulted in certain locomotives being fitted with a single buffing plate between locomotive and tender; for many years Ryecroft's 28088, 28105, 28246, 28247 and 28251 were to be seen on the branch, these examples noted above being so fitted. A further problem was fractured feed hoses from the tender for water supply to the boiler. This was overcome by fitting specially designed and strengthened hoses which were unaffected by the sheer on the tight curves. The gallant five locomotives consequently remained Ryecroft engines for the rest of their working lives. After the 1923 grouping some Johnson-designed Midland 2Fs were used, the type replacing the Webbs as they were withdrawn from service, until the branch closure in 1964. The coal engines could only manage a few wagons at a time and so had to make several trips to make up a train, colliery subsidence also badly affecting the rollercoaster ride. The durable little 0-6-0s had their limitations. Their braking capacity certainly left something to be desired so activity on the branch often necessitated a fitter's visit to rectify mishaps. Ryecroft's Frank Rigby, a fitter in the 1930s, recalls many visits to retrieve lost buffer planks, bolted to the engine frame by four large bolts. One severe snatch with the loose coupled wagons could rip the buffer plank from the engine, the locomotive then having to proceed to Ryecroft with pulley blocks from the chimney supporting the damaged plank. Engine and wagon derailments were frequent but, fortunately, nothing really serious was experienced and re-railing became a fine art.

Bescot men had the worst of the shunt, most of their shift being during the night. The darkness has its advantages, though, as Bescot driver Reg Share relates. During 'snap' (break) time, about 9.30 p.m., the routine was to park the locomotive in the cutting at Shelfield to retire to the local public house. On one dark winter's night, he and his mate returned to the engine to find a gang of schoolchildren on the footplate trying to get the locomotive in motion. The following night the regulator handle was unscrewed and hidden in a grass embankment. After their cheese sandwich and a pint supper, on leaving the pub they encountered quite a thick fog and it proved quite difficult to find the vital part, even after a frantic search. If it had not been found, a locomotive foreman would need to be told of the lost regulator and the circumstances surrounding it. The air would have been blue with choice language, the incident would probably have created a small chapter in railway history, and far more paperwork than was liked!

Reg Share vividly recalls the complicated shunt manoeuvre by night, taking the loaded wagons over the hump-backed canal bridge, the gradient on both sides being 1 in 75 or steeper. On a wet night the charging coal engine, fully opened out, often lost its grip, the resultant wheelslip providing an extremely noisy pyrotechnic display which enhanced the glow and glare of the brickyard's coal-fired kilns. The exhausting locomotive added to the clouds of rolling smoke from the brooding column chimneys, the whole area in the shadow and lights of Leighswood Colliery as its steam-winding gear emitted strange moans and hissing noises throughout the night. Ryecroft's tenure of duty was less sinister, consisting of journeys to take several loaded brick wagons to the extensive siding by Leighswood Junction signal box, to make up full trains. Sometimes these wagons were added to passing long-distance freights, their already considerable trains being bound for various destinations. The view from the box was, until about 1950, distinctly rural, with cattle grazing in the nearby meadows, at peace and contented until disturbed by a charging 'goods engine'. The trips to Leighswood sidings helped to break the monotony in both brickyard and colliery, the limit for the journeys being fifteen loads. A network of sidings abounded to service and forward some of the considerable coal and brick production to the Midland Railway line between Aldridge and Brownhills. This output was shunted into a long siding parallel with the mainline, for the Midland locomotives to collect. In pre-grouping days, L&NWR engines never ventured on to the Aldridge–Brownhills line.

Every railway has its moments, and Ryecroft driver Sid Hadley recalls one particular tense moment on the Leighswood duty. One day Ryecroft allocated a 'Cauliflower' 18in goods 0-6-0 to the Leighswood shunt which, with its larger driving wheels and consequent higher boiler centre line, caused some consternation. The mixed traffic 0-6-0 was peacefully trundling towards the brickworks on the first trip of empty wagons. On reaching the bridge at the Lichfield Road, Shelfield, the crew felt a jolt and loud crash with falling brickwork onto the boiler. Coming to a halt in a dense cloud of dust, the 'Cauliflower' was minus its chimney. It is not known why the 'Cauliflower' was working this trip, but it is possible that the 18in goods was being trialled for comparison purposes to see if there were any traction advantage over the usual 17in goods. It was never adopted. The old Webb engine's driver, Frank Ash, had very little to report on the incident, except

The Leighswood shunt, 8 September 1953. This is Lichfield Road bridge where a Ryecroft 'Cauliflower' lost its chimney. (F.W. Shuttleworth)

that the bridge suffered from sudden subsidence and head-butted his engine. The bridge had damaged itself.

The largest engine ever to traverse the branch came during the great snow of 1940 when the Cannock line was completely snowbound by huge drifts, five engines being stranded for five days. This story was repeated over a wide area of the West Midlands. The most suitable locomotive for snow plough use was, of course, the ubiquitous 'Super D' 0-8-0. For some days a plough engine and a similar helper toured all the lines radiating from Bescot, the principal shed in the area. It took a long time to clear each branch and their respective sidings and when Leighswood's turn came, Sid Hadley was the driver. On approaching Leighswood sidings after a stint at Norton Junction, the thought arose that an 0-8-0 had never used the branch before. After a long consultation with 'control' via Leighswood signal box, permission was granted for the plough-fitted 'D' to proceed with caution. With its chimney clearing the bridges by inches, the clearing went ahead, the only time an 0-8-0 worked on the branch.

During the 1930s the two collieries closed and the branch was used solely for the brick and tile trade. One recalls the wagons filled with tiles neatly packed in wooden boxes lined with straw, the wagons carrying warning labels worded 'shunt with care'. Post-1945 the tile works found that the motor lorry was a more convenient way of delivering its output, as once loaded they were delivered straight to the customer's site. Reserves of clay were also rapidly diminishing. Although vast quantities of clay remained to be mined, the reserves had been built over, mining extension obviously being ruled out, and by 1977 only one brickworks remained open. Leighswood signal box, the sidings and the branch were closed in 1964, the box being demolished shortly afterwards and the track removed. Shelfield cutting was filled with hardcore and new houses have now been built on parts of the track.

There is now little trace of this extremely busy branch line which served a highly intensive extraction industry so typical of the West Midlands, brick, clay and old King coal.

The whole length of the branch was worked by token from Leighswood Signal box, the token being round and painted red. To proceed beyond the box the locomotive crew acquired the token, and the guard a ticket. This ensured only one engine could be in a 'section' at any one time. Trains from Aldridge Colliery to Leighswood were required to come to a halt adjacent to Coppy Hall Sidings for the guard to apply wagon brakes at the Shelfield main road bridge. (Information on token operation from Ernie Genders, a Bescot fireman.)

The Bridgeman Place and Long Street Goods Yard Shunt

This shunt was probably the busiest shunt. It worked the Long Street area from Bridgeman Place and Walsall Station. It served the L&NWR Long Street and GWR (Great Western Railway) covered goods deck, which covered an area to Corporation Street bridge. This area was always known as Bodley's and was named after farmer George Bodley who sold the land to the railway company. It was adjacent to Walsall No.1 signal box. The traffic was so busy that a shunt engine was required at each end of the yard. It was a twenty-four-hour duty, but sometimes the night shift would be reduced if daytime shunting went to plan. If the Bridgeman Place shunter was available it would take wagons to Ryecroft shed to assist in a shunting turn known as the Brewer's shunt. This shunt was a very complicated shunt by virtue of having to cross both up and down mainlines between Butts bridge and St Paul's cutting. The one siding which came off the down slow lines ran, in L&NWR days, to serve Brewers limestone works near the Lime House – residence of Oscar Johnson and family. The siding was also used by a timberyard around the turn of the century. A siding was laid to serve the Hatherton Street factories of The Oak Tanning Co., Nevilles Foundry, Hales Timberyard and Brooks and Ortons Timberyard. The shunts serving all these businesses were always referred to by Ryecroft men as the Brewer's shunt. The siding to these factories ran off the up fast mainline. Owing to the vicinity of the Fordbrook River, access to this siding was halfway between Butts bridge and Littleton Street bridge. To shunt wagons onto this siding, the locomotive had to position the wagons for Oak Tanning one end, with the rest attached to the chimney end, and to make up the train in this order it had to retire to the Ryecroft shed confines. This incurred the wrath of the Ryecroft shed staff for interfering with a busy schedule. When timing the moves into Brewers sidings, with passenger and freight trains passing.every few minutes, the problems faced by the shed staff were nothing when compared to the trials of Ryecroft Junction's signalmen. Accomodating this shunt engine within their already tight margins must have been a nightmare. In heavy traffic conditions the shunt would be worked at night, but finding a path across the lines was still not easy, even after the passenger trains had ceased running – a constant procession of mineral and goods trains bringing no respite for the double-manned Ryecroft signalmen. All wagons returning from Brewer's shunt were returned to Bridgeman Place or Bodley's Long Street goods yard.

Loco 8088 in Walsall shunting transfer freight from ex-LNWR sidings to the ex-Midland railway sidings, 1936. (John Bucknall Collection)

The Birchills Shunt

The Birchills shunt was very popular because of its working hours. The Ryecroft men booked on at 7.00 a.m. and ran a light engine to Bridgeman Place to pick up a small train for Birchills sidings and Talbot Stead Tube works. Originally in L&NWR days, this shunt served the Birchills Hall Ironworks. In the 1930s the large Talbot Stead Tube works required a weekday shunt, and the nearby timberyard of Parker & Sons, Green Lane, had a regular delivery of tree trunks. A siding into Moseley's coal yard in Bloxwich Road demanded a daily quota of household coal. After midday the shunt would be completed when the shunt engine, with its load of tubes for overseas and British markets, would take a short trip to Bloxwich. Here it would make up Bloxwich yard's daily despatches into a short-trip freight back to Bridgeman Place, leaving at about 4.30 p.m. The Birchills shunt became very busy during the Second World War, as Talbot Stead's output increased with regular deliveries of raw steel for tube making and new sidings were laid on the site of the Old Birchills Ironworks. Four mobile steam cranes were required to load and unload wagons, and also to shunt wagons, despite their limited speed of 4mph at full throttle. An added wartime task for the Birchills shunt was to leave petrol tanks at the rear of Birchills' bus depot to save delivery by road. Also during wartime the Birchills shunt engine would, if required, run to Bloxwich for shunting assistance. Normally, Bloxwich relied on passing trip freight engines to assist their shunting requirements. Because of the sociable timings allocated to this duty, it was known amongst the men as an 'office hours' duty.

Loco off Talbot Stead shunt passing Ryecroft shed at a time when the duty was operated by Bescot shed, 1962. (Jack Haddock Collection)

The Holly Bank Shunt

A Ryecroft engine would be working the Holly Bank shunt from about 6.00 a.m. until 6.00 p.m. The shunt dealt with coal from the Holly Bank and Hilton Main collieries close to Essington, and also the Rosemary Tiles factory in Bursnips Road, Essington. The first part of the day consisted of moving empty mineral wagons from the Essington Wood sidings near Broad Lane, which was 1 mile from Bloxwich station (a short way north of the present day Mossley Estate), to sidings at Bursnips Road. Loaded wagons would then return to Essington Wood sidings with several trips between these sidings being undertaken daily. Passing freights on the main Walsall to Cannock line attached and detached mineral wagons to keep the Holly Bank shunter busy. The daily traffic out of Holly Bank Colliery was immense; the Hilton Main colliery's output was brought to Holly Bank over a private line about 3 miles in length by the resident pits' shunting engines. The demarcation line was the level crossing on Bursnips Road and at this point one must mention the unusual signal box attached to one of the colliery's buildings. It operated two large poles that dropped across the main road, plus signals each side of the crossing. Fortunately, photographs survive of this unique signal box. Even more fortunate is that it can still be seen today. Its present owners have sympathetically restored what became a very rundown building, to its former glory. It still stands as a sentinel to the past next to the overbridge spanning the M6.

Colliery engines were allowed over the crossing to the Bursnips Road sidings but not down to Essington Wood sidings, and the Ryecroft shunter was only allowed over the crossing to the colliery water column. No water facilities were available at Essington Wood sidings. The Ryecroft driver was then issued with a chit to be presented to Ryecroft Shed's office. This was, in fact, a bill from the colliery, thus charging for their water. By

Holly Bank Colliery loco crossing Bursnips Road with a train of coal to exchange sidings at Essington on the Cannock line, 1930s. (Stanley Webb)

Holly Bank Colliery loco crossing Bursnips Road with a train of coal to exchange sidings at Essington on the Cannock line, showing to better effect the distinctive signal box. (R. Jeavons)

mid-afternoon the Ryecroft shunter had finished its coal movements. It then ran along a very rural line through woods and fields to the then productive Rosemary Tiles factory, once again crossing Bursnips Road, but about 1 mile further north. Its final job was to bring the day's tile production of about ten loaded flat wagons, back to Essington Wood. These tiles would all be packed in straw-lined cases, with each wagon displaying a large sign saying 'shunt with care'. The Holly Bank shunter would then run to Bridgeman Place at a sedate pace, and eventually retire back to Ryecroft Shed.

8

The Double Trip Link

The double trip link was manned by volunteers as this necessitated lodging away from home, but they were financially rewarded by its longer working hours. The top job in this link, the Walsall to Camden Town goods, the 'Camdens' as the job was known, started from Long Street goods yard and picked up at Bescot and Stechford, then ran express to Camden. The Wellingborough double trip originated from the Midland Timber yard in Tasker Street, Walsall, to its destination. This duty was acquired from the Midland after the 1923 grouping and involved picking up at Water Orton, Nuneaton and Wigston. It was a duty noted for its overtime, sometimes taking over twelve hours on the foot plate. The protracted nature of this job could result in crews being relieved after fifteen hours in both directions and was a highly used service. The final duty in this link was the 20 miles only, double-trip run to Stafford which is fully examined in a section of its own. It was notorious for being the shortest double-trip lodging duty operated in this country. The return journey always diverted at East Cannock Junction to traverse the branch line to Norton Junction, where the duty terminated.

Ryecroft Shed Double Trip Link – Walsall To Stafford

The double-trip working from Walsall to Stafford, worked by Ryecroft and Stafford sheds, was possibly the shortest double-trip turn on any British Railway; the distance being only 20 miles. The Ryecroft men had to spend a night in Stafford shed barracks as they could not get home due to lack of rail connections. The Stafford crews, however, were able to return to base and avoid lodging out. For train crews visiting Ryecroft, certain local houses were available offering bed and breakfast. Most of these belonged to Ryecroft men, the families accepting their visitors and their lodging-out allowances to help with housekeeping costs. In the 1930s era this was approximately 3*s* 6*d* per night.

Left: Ryecroft shed mess room with driver Fred Haywood and mates playing cards, Christmas Day, 1963. (Jack Haddock Collection)

Colliery loco at Hawkins Colliery situated near Churchbridge on the Cannock line. This colliery was serviced by the Stafford double trip link. (John Bucknall Collection)

In L&NWR days the Staffords were hauled by a Webb 0-6-0 coal engine or 'Cauliflower', and generally in the LMS era by a Super D 0-8-0. The turn was, in reality, a travelling interchange shunt setting off from Bridgeman Place Sidings at 11.28 a.m. The first stop was at Birchills Sidings for the extensive Talbot Stead steel tube works on the Cannock Branch. It was accessed by a short, sharp, curving reversal which was situated near to where Green Lane crosses the line. The train would go into the yard to detach, shunt and assemble ready-loaded trucks for onward passage. As a teenager, my daily journey to a Walsall school by bus seldom witnessed actual activity, most journeys marked by a simmering coal engine at rest, probably while tubes were being loaded for despatch. The train when made up often had to wait for a considerable time due to local passenger services and the constant procession of empty wagons being sent to Hednesford yard to load the black diamonds mined by the several collieries on Cannock Chase. Production from these pits totalled several million tons annually. Once a road was available, the train undertook a short, steep climb to a plateau at Bloxwich and its busy yard. Although only a small yard with a one-road covered, decked storage and interchange facility, two horse-drawn drays were kept busy delivering produce and goods to many local businesses. The wagons delivered to outlying districts like Essington and New Invention, as well as Bloxwich itself, which was, and still is, a busy little town centred around a bustling High Street shopping area. A busy timber yard demanded a regular supply of trees and ready-sawn timber, while the town was serviced by two coal merchants. Next stop was about a mile north at Essington Wood Sidings to service Holly Bank and Hilton Main collieries, their locomotives being used to transport empty and full wagons to and from the interchange sidings. Leaving Essington, the line dropped a further 1.5 miles to Great Wyrley, where a spur dropped off steeply to cross the road to Cheslyn Hay by a level crossing, the single line servicing Hawkins Colliery and also a rail/canal interchange facility at Churchbridge on the A5

Watling Street; some 1.5 miles from Cannock. Mid Cannock Colliery was situated at Churchbridge, and a short distance further north was Cannock station which overlooked the town's gas works, itself a considerable consumer of coal, with coke being produced as a by-product of the production of pungent-smelling 'Town Gas'. Another large user of rail was Wootton's very considerable timber yard near to the station's own busy interchange, storage and despatch facility. This was kept busy by commercial demands of the town and its hinterland. Some 3 miles away, Hednesford was reached by a continuing steep climb, passing East Cannock Junction on the way. This is where the connection from the Norton collieries joined the route. It was common for up to three hours to be spent at Hednesford, despite there being a resident shunt engine supplied by Ryecroft. East of Hednesford, West Cannock Colliery would be passed without the need to carry out any work, as the trainloads of coal from this concern were dealt with by the resident shunter at Hednesford. The next activity would be at the Brereton Colliery complex and their interchange sidings at Rugeley, beside Brereton Colliery signal box. The 'Staffords' usually rolled past, again leaving the coal trains to other scheduled services, and made for the important junction at Rugeley Trent Valley on the Euston to Glasgow mainline (often referred to as the 'Trent Valley' route). Here a protracted shunting stint could be the cause of further delays. The line was four track as it made for Colwich, where the Stoke-On-Trent 'cut off' branched right, leaving a heavily used two-track section to Milford. Here the Trent Valley route was overlooked by the rapidly rising Cannock Chase, which necessitated the boring of the 777-yard Shugbrugh Tunnel, with its ornamental North Portal demanded by the Anson family, through whose beautifully laid-out sylvan estate the railway was built. The constant passage of mainline expresses plus fast and local freight services at the two-track constriction, made it a matter of luck for an early passage of the 'Staffords', any hold up becoming a frustration as the trains destination was almost in sight.

Leaving the tunnel, the line curved into Milford, where the station's shunt was a fairly easy proposition. In times past it was considerably more hectic here, as supplies and military essentials would be transferred to a service railway line that ran to the military camps on the high Chase plateau. The line originating by West Cannock Colliery, Hednesford, never had any direct connection to the mainline at Milford, so interchange was labour intensive

The short romp to Stafford was made easier by the four-track layout north of Milford. Just before Stafford, the salt works would be serviced in the return up direction, leaving only the British Reinforced Concrete Co. sidings opposite Queensville signal box, to be shunted before reaching the Queensville curve and the entry to Stafford. Shunting at the British Reinforced Concrete Co.'s yard was usually considered a Stafford Shed (5C) duty. With such a complex set of facilities to be visited by the double-home job, the normal on-time arrival at Stafford was often overrun. The 9.30 p.m. booked arrival in reality often came much later. Conditions on Cannock Chase also played their part – time would often be lost in very adverse weather conditions.

On arrival at Stafford, the Ryecroft men had time for a drink and meal before retiring to their overnight accommodation in the barracks at the west side of the locomotive depot. Here they would be woken in the morning, in time to meet their return trip departure at 7.45 a.m. The return trip followed a similar but reversed procedure shunting and interchanging wagons at the same goods yards and sometimes at the salt works, until after the Hednesford yard shunt. On leaving Hednesford and passing an important wagon repair and construction facility on the right, the train headed towards Cannock but took a left-hand diversion onto the Norton branch at East Cannock Junction to shunt at Littleworth Colliery sidings. From here the train was worked under the 'train staff token system', over the single-line section to Norton Crossing. Coal was normally the only commodity to be shunted in this area. From Norton Crossing to Norton Junction, permissive block working was the rule, trains queueing up behind each other until their turn to be hump shunted at Norton Junction sidings arrived (see chapter 7.)

This was, essentially, the end of the duty, with the Norton Junction hump shunter sorting out the train and its wagons being reassembled into other configurations for onward transit to a wide variety of destinations. The Ryecroft engine would thus be released to run light engine to its Walsall shed, but could be used in times of necessity to flat shunt at the Pelsall side of the sidings. In adverse winter or foggy conditions, if there was a need for flat shunting the crew would be relieved and allowed to make their own way back to book off at Ryecroft shed. They would hitch a lift aboard one of the many mineral trains passing in the up direction.

The Ryecroft double-trip link was staffed by volunteer drivers, the heavier weekly pay packet being considered more important than the unsociable hours and overnight absence involved. This strange train tended to produce regular footplate pairings, where any mismatching of personalities was potentially catastrophic, but then the spirit of Ryecroft adventure never got as far as Russian roulette.

9

The Special Link

In steam days Ryecroft had a link for special duties and came under the overall jurisdiction of the main Midland area control link at Birmingham New Street station. It could be considered a type of strategic reserve. Crews in this link could have anything thrown at them, or be expected to go almost anywhere. In pre-war days, the occupant of a post in a special link could be expected to remain at home (usually close to the shed) for up to ten hours on call. This made havoc of a day (or night) if a call out came late in unpaid time. In general, the major shed at Bescot dealt with derailments with its allocated steam crane, but failed locomotives or workhorses needing assistance came under 'specials' provision. The ideal driver was someone like E.R. Hughes, who was passed for an extremely wide range of operations and was qualified to go pretty well anywhere. In the late 1940s and early 1950s, Ken Horan fired for Eddy in this link and recalls a call out to the Coventry area to relieve a crew bringing up the immaculate Britannia Pacific locomotive, 70004 *William Shakespeare*. It had spent a period on exhibition as part of the Festival of Britain at Battersea Park, and this was its return journey to Crewe light engine. The almost new engine rode beautifully; Ken had little to do as far as firing was concerned, and enjoyed the mainly seated job in a spotlessly clean and painted cab. Eddy soon mastered the glorious chime whistle to good effect, announcing his passing of every signal box with a beautiful 'whip poor will' wail that would have been applauded on any American line. On depositing the beauty on Crewe North shed, the pair had a break and then brought back a troop train special to Birmingham, where they ended their highly individual and enjoyable duty. The pair had a long and successful foot plate partnership; Eddy, as a senior driver, probably pulled a few strings to keep a good mate. Special link dedication often resulted in spare time on shed awaiting a job, but a break was sometimes enjoyed at Tommy Deakins (the Royal Exchange) in nearby Mill Street. If anything came up the duty foreman would send across a cleaner or knock-up lad which interrupted the relaxation and soft drinks! Other typical special link work was the evening excursions and special race trains to Perry Barr, Birmingham, for the greyhound racing and, more often, the speedway. This involved two outward journeys from Walsall, parking

Ryecroft shed control office, 1952. (Joe Parr)

the stock at Vauxhall after the second and two Perry Barr to Walsalls at the end of the meetings.

Ryecroft Trip Specials

Fishermen's Specials

During early LMS years the company experimented with special services to attract extra fare-paying passengers. One of these ventures, recalled by retired Ryecroft drivers, involved the local fishermen's specials. These ran on Sundays during the appropriate fishing season, and became very popular. Ryecroft worked a fishermen's train starting in the early hours of the morning from Rugeley to Shrewsbury via Walsall, Wolverhampton, Stafford and Wellington. Once established, it attracted so many anglers and their families that a nine-coach train of non-corridor local stock was needed, the special calling at all stations en route to enable fishermen to make their way to local canals and the rivers Penk and Sow. The majority went to Shrewsbury, its attraction being the fabled river Severn. The most suitable power was found to be the Midland Class 3 0-6-0s with their large capacity tenders, to ensure an adequate supply of water throughout the day. Nos 3333, 3410 and 3502 were regularly used on the service. On arrival at Shrewsbury, the locomotive retired to the shed for servicing. The 3C men did not relish the hard water supply in the Stafford and Shrewsbury areas which would cause 'priming' if care was not taken. When an engine braked sharply, it could cause a wave effect along the boiler, allowing water into the steam-collecting apparatus, and hence into the cylinders. This would be deposited as dirty water droplets on prospective passengers, who could then claim compensation for soiled clothing. The higher proportion of insolubles in the water supply, if not treated, could also affect the boiler's steaming potential.

The specials which ran during the Depression years were a boon for the Ryecroft men, being an extra job with long Sunday hours and ideal for the pay packet. With the advent of hostilities the services were withdrawn and, unfortunately, were not reintroduced after 1945. During the late 1940s and early '50s the Motor Coach provided a more personal service delivering fishermen direct to the river bank or suitable canalside – a real benefit as items such as heavy rods, tackle, keep nets and wicker baskets would otherwise have to be carried on a lengthy walk from the stations. The natural evolution of the fishermen's service was finally played out, as increasing prosperity saw a vast surge in the numbers of private cars on the road, leading to the demise of the bus and coach as a means of leisure transport. The ultimate flexibility was your own steering wheel, an Ordnance Survey map and a wandering spirit, which in combination sounded the death knell of 'awayday' fishing by train, and the end of the 'Fish-ex' ticket.

Whit Monday Specials to Lichfield Bower

Whit Monday Bank Holiday at Lichfield City station was always the busiest day of the year. I calculate that special trains to the 'Lichfield Bower' originated shortly after the South Staffordshire line opened through to Lichfield in 1849. As these notes concern the working of trains by crews from Ryecroft shed, I am relating the memories of now-retired Ryecroft drivers. Those men who were of an age to have worked for the L&NWR, confirm that Ryecroft always provided about five excursion trains to Lichfield, in order that the citizens of Walsall and other towns and villages on the route of the railway could make their way to the 'Bower'. The number of excursions that actually ran was dependent on the weather conditions on the day. A boiling hot summer's day would bring immense crowds to Walsall station. As with other excursions, the Walsall stationmaster would have matters well in hand. In the early morning, locomotives and crews with about nine coach trains would follow each other out of Walsall at regular intervals. The local stationmasters en route to Lichfield would inform Walsall of their crowd situation, and certain trains would leave empty to deal with these passengers. Ryecroft drivers recall running into Pelsall and Brownhills and seeing the platforms full to capacity. I am told by Pelsall senior citizens that before the advent of motor bus transport, people from surrounding villages walked miles to Pelsall or Brownhills for the train to the 'Bower'.

It must be mentioned that Ryecroft was not the only supplier of trains for the 'Bower'. Visitors flocked in on excursions from Burton-on-Trent and Birmingham New Street as well. In the days before efficient road transport, say up until about 1930, most people made their way to Lichfield by train. The road to Lichfield would only have a handful of early motor cars, some people in ponies and traps, a number of cyclists and, of course, those on foot. People did not mind walking a few miles in those days! With excursions arriving at Lichfield City from three directions, it was necessary for the L&NWR and later the LMS, to appoint a railway controller from the Midland area office to be based at Lichfield City for this one-day operation. He alone was reponsible for ensuring complete harmony without disrupting the normal passenger train timetable.

It is fair to say that at no time did these Whit Monday excursions cause any chaos or hold up. As the years progressed, the railway companies learned from experience and formed a controlled routine. The Ryecroft men only remember being held up at signals on the approach to Lichfield City for a few minutes at a time. The one concern during this operation for engine drivers was the water supply at Lichfield City. There were no water columns here. The main facilities were at Lichfield Trent Valley High Level, consisting of a high, bricked-up tank situated on the down line on the Burton side of the station. There was also a parachute-type tank on the up line, on the Lichfield City side of the station. As most local trains from Walsall and Birmingham usually ran down to Trent Valley to connect with trains on the low-level mainline, they always took on water there. There was an emergency water supply at Lichfield City in the form of a water hydrant, situated between platforms 2 and 3, complete with a length of fire hose.

Most of the locomotives for these 'Bower' specials were tender engines after the 1923 grouping, because of their greater water capacity. Until the advent of the Second World War, Ryecroft Super Ds and Midland Class 4s were the mainstay of the 'Bower' specials. From this point on, traffic to the 'Bower' began to decline – probably due to the upsurge in road transport that was available – and the specials were doomed. The buses gradually won over a lot of trippers to the 'Bower', with their lower prices and more convenient pick-up points. An increase in car ownership through the 1950s, coupled with rising fares on the railway, eventually led British Railways to cease running to the 'Bower' from about 1964 onwards. Ryecroft closed to steam in 1957, thus for their last few years the specials were worked by diesel multiple units. From 1964 Walsall Corporation Transport ran extra buses on the No.16 Walsall to Lichfield route, but at the time of writing these notes, this too, has ceased.

Specials Walsall to Perry Barr and Walsall to Sutton Park

After a long, hard day's work in the many local factories, the citizens of Walsall relished their leisure time. The railway, of course, was always willing to find a means to deliver them to their chosen destination. Only a few miles away, at Perry Barr, was the dog-racing stadium, as it still is today. The attraction was a flutter on the dogs. Many Walsall families kept dogs as pets, mainly Staffordshire Bull Terriers, Whippets and Greyhounds, while small Terrier breeds, especially Jack Russells, were more suited to the smaller homes. Some had their dogs in training, hoping to produce a winner, but unfortunately most greyhounds performed well below the levels required for serious winnings. Optimism abounded, though, and a few quid won by racing or robbing the bookie was always welcome.

Ryecroft provided for this traffic using one six-car train doing two journeys on race nights, usually in the capable hands of a Stanier 2-6-4T. Ken Horan undertook firing duties to his regular mate Eddie Hughes on some of these trips, and although not heavy work, run-rounds had to be made at both Walsall and Perry Barr. The bulk of the time seemed to be taken coupling and uncoupling, changing lamps and brake tests. After the second trip, the empty set was sent to Vauxhall carriage sidings to wait time for the first pick up on a return run to Walsall, after the racing had finished. A short walk enabled liquid refreshment to be taken during the racing and a couple to be downed with a game of darts or crib, or just a relaxed chat and fresh air. All in all, a nice little earner, fairly light firing and a modest schedule or, in Ken's terms, 'taking the smooth with the rough'. It is very surprising how many locomotive sheds had public houses built not far from the shed gates. Drinking on duty, of course, was officially banned.

A more arduous turn was operated to Sutton Park on summer Sundays. Again, one locomotive and a six- or eight-car set performed the duty over a steeply graded route. From Walsall to the Streetly and Aldridge stops were uphill, then downhill to the park. The duty required hard firing uphill, the downhill providing respite time to tidy up the footplate and fill up the boiler. This duty amounted to eight Walsall to Sutton Park returns, each tightly timed with the same repetitive duties carried out sixteen times during the day's work. With a demanding schedule which denied any possibility or availability of a watering hole, there was no respite for the hard-working crew.

Water could be taken at Walsall as required. The 2-6-4T was easy to run either forwards or backwards, providing a good ride and a punchy performance. Not considered an easy duty, it was, however, rewarding in the pocket. After the long, dry day, it was the crew's turn to fill up the tanks, and Eddie liked more than one or two. Although he had his preferred drinking places, after parking the stock and returning light engine to Ryecroft, the first open hostelry outside the shed confines would be thankfully visited.

Sutton Park's attraction was its wide open spaces for leisure, games or picnics. There was a large resident fun-fair operated by Pat Collins (who late in life became mayor of Walsall), a superb miniature railway, two large boating lakes and several tea rooms. All attractions were well used for Sunday school outings, club and party visits. Sutton Park was host to the huge Worldwide Scout Jubilee Jamboree held in August 1957, to celebrate fifty years (1907–57) of International Scouting Worldwide. A set of British commemorative stamps was issued on 1 August 1957 to mark the occasion. An enhanced regular train service for visitors and Scouts was run throughout the Jamboree, and for arrival and dispersal of the Scouts and their equipment.

Special Trips – Brighton

After the 1923 grouping, the limit of Ryecroft's sphere of activity was to Euston, Bristol, Bath, Weston Super Mare, Derby, Shrewsbury, Blackpool and the North Wales resorts. Wellingborough via Wigston was also acquired as a freight route. After nationalisation of the railways in 1948, a number of special trips were undertaken on an experimental basis, mainly to widen provision for summer seaside excursion traffic. After the end of hostilities, a travel-starved public were eager to get to the seaside for their annual holidays. At this time, this regular exodus tested rail facilities to the full, although later on, the railways would suffer intense competition from the long-distance coach and, as post-war prosperity increased, the private car. Almost all top-link drivers at Ryecroft knew the road to Blackpool and the North Wales coast, and looked forward to the intense summer excursion traffic to enhance their earnings.

A Southern region penetration, acquired by Ryecroft in the immediate post-war period in 1950, was to prove eventful. Three special trains were utilised, organised by the Whitton Allotment Committee, their destination being Brighton. Ryecroft men were familiar with the road to Willesden Junction, Southern men taking over from there to

45308 coming on shed in 1955. This was the loco that almost came to grief after leaving Brighton due to inferior coal supply. (Jack Haddock Collection)

the coast via Kensington Olympia and Clapham Junction. The locomotives allocated were 3 Stanier 'Black Fives', Ryecroft men recollecting their numbers as 44873, 45308 and 45416. Driver Jim Barnet recalled his trials and tribulations on the footplate of 45308, incidentally shared by his mates aboard the other 5s. The trip to Brighton was uneventful and uninteresting. Jim could have travelled on the cushions but chose to familiarise his Southern counterpart with the finer points of Class 5 running. The new crew relished the opportunity to handle the Stanier, a type not based on the former Southern region. By remaining on the footplate, the Ryecroft crew were able to view a completely new road, and one which had its dangers due to third rail electrification – a challenging journey of discovery. On arrival at Brighton, disposal men took over the 5s, whose crews booked off and after a wash and a meal chose to sample the South Coast sea and air. After servicing the locomotives, the disposal crews coaled the 5s, the bunkered fuel supply at Brighton at that time being in the form of 2-3in-diameter briquettes which were being trialled with the aim of improving steaming capacities. With 5s seldom, if ever, reaching Brighton, the shed's disposal staff placed their charges on the allocated road for the afternoon stay, and in Southern tradition filled the fireboxes to capacity with briquettes. They then closed the damper and left the 5s to simmer until the Ryecroft men returned some six hours later. They were confronted with fireboxes filled to capacity, and the briquettes fused together into a huge block of clinker, with boiler pressure very low. Jim, his mate and the other 3C men had to work frantically to break the solid mass within the firebox. With the aid of the blower it was a struggle to raise steam pressure as departure time approached to pick up the stock. When the Southern pilot crews arrived, they could see the visitor's predicament, and piled in with welcome help and muscle.

Their combined efforts managed to get air into the mass to aid combustion, but even so, by the time 45308 departed from Brighton, steam was barely adequate. They somehow got to Willesden with locomotives that lacked the usual Class 5 sparkle, their arrival being somewhat late. With briquettes loaded at Brighton to top up the tender, very little could be done to improve the situation until this supply had been burnt off. The constant battle for steam was waged between Willesden and Rugby by feeding the briquettes little and often, the fireman foraging in the depths of the tender to mine a seam of 'real' coal. With the briquettes consumed and the remains of the original supply available, the ailing 5 was restored to near normal. Steam pressure was again at blowing-off point as Aston was approached. After all three specials deposited their empty stock in Midland Road carriage sidings, the locomotives returned to Ryecroft. Their crews were no doubt in a mood to compare notes (and expletives) when discussing the merits of the experimental fuel. For the valiant crews who had struggled to provide a great day for the passengers in their charge, the verdict on their Brighton 'rock' was a unanimous thumbs down. It was demanded that for the future, each 5 was to be equipped with two tenders full of real coal should the Brighton destination be tried again. Once bitten! Valuable lessons had been learned for further trips to foreign regions on special trains.

10

The Disposal Link

Although self preparation of a locomotive was quite common, at the end of a turn of duty the mount was driven onto the shed and handed over to the disposal link for fire cleaning or dropping, coaling, watering and the cleaning of smoke box char. The locomotive would then be positioned for servicing, repair or cleaning, on its allocated road either inside or outside the shed. The shift was not timed, its requirement being to dispose of eight locomotives before home time. With round-the-clock operations, several teams would be started at various times in the twenty-four-hour cycle. There could obviously be times of great pressure and slack depending on incoming traffic. After signing-on at 2 p.m., it was sometimes possible to have seven under the belt by 5 p.m. If another machine came in quickly you were lucky – an early finish. If not, your duty ended after your eighth cycle, whenever that was achieved. If you started at a slack time you could end up with a very long shift.

Disposal was an opportunity to introduce young men to the foot plate after the rigours of a long, protracted spell of cleaning. Usually the senior of the pair was responsible for driving the loco on shed; his younger colleague picked up the know-how and would eventually be able to drive himself, at a very restricted speed, of course. The downside of the coin was the filthy side of the job, where fire and ash disposal regimes, clinker breaking and smoke box duties produced clouds of smoke and dust which was made worse in high swirling winds. Ken Horan recalls a wild west ride he had on a super 'D' 0-8-0 on disposal duties. The incoming driver had not opened the cocks to drain any steam in the cylinders so, as Ken opened the regulator to move forward and shutting it almost immediately, the 'D' shot away in forward gear with such continuous energy that even a brake application did not work. A very frightened young man was being unwillingly carried across the turntable and beyond, where well-placed buffers braced and ready, were given a belt which could be heard all over the shed, even in Mr Heap's office. Out rushed the shed master, gesticulating and moving fast. Ken got roasted for someone else's mistake.

Not linked were the special artisan trades for locomotive maintenance and repair, all requiring engineering and metals skills to keep locomotives on the road. Specialist

Shed view with 49158 on disposal line, showing the ash plant coaling stage, 1957. (F.W. Shuttleworth)

wheelwrights, boiler men, brick-arch builders, a blacksmith and several maintenance fitters were on Ryecroft's books, often having mates. These were young men learning the trade and providing an extra pair of hands.

The planning of all links was the preserve of the shed master, next week's rota being pinned up at midday on Saturday, before the top man performed a strategic retreat in the direction of home. This would leave the running shift foreman to deal with any problems. The principal grouse was the allocation of locomotives known to be steaming badly, or mechanically run-down examples awaiting shopping, to duties which lasted for the week. Others typically swore there was favouritism, or too many night turns, or too few of the most financially rewarding jobs. On the whole, the system was accepted by all but the perennial grouses – it had to be. These men had their say but were summarily dismissed, and told where to go by the foreman whose main armament was a thick skin and a deaf ear (or two).

The unofficial brotherhood of call-up lads were also allocated to duties in shifts, and covered the Butts, Ryecroft and the more distant Leamore areas. Passing along Coalpool Lane opposite the cemetery, some strange apparitions could await the unwary at night, as the shed's jokers tested the guts, resolve and fitness of young men employed to wake the shed's living 'dead' from their beds. The result of the haunting would quickly be circulated on the shed's grapevine, the grim story embroidered at every telling. Ryecroft enjoyed its fun, never vicious, but with few holds barred.

11

The Bug

Before Bescot sidings and running shed were opened, most of the Black Country rail traffic was operated by steam locomotives from Aston, Monument Lane, or Ryecroft sheds within the L&NWR system. Ryecroft was more or less responsible for most of the old 'South Staffordshire' lines from Dudley to Wychnor Junction, operating both passenger and freight. After Bescot shed was opened in 1892, to help with the growing demand for Black Country freight traffic, Ryecroft shed gradually took over the local passenger services leaving Bescot as essentially a freight shed, but until 1918 Ryecroft retained one shunt duty within the confines of the large Great Bridge goods yard. Ryecroft also continued to undertake freight duties and was also responsible for some ten local shunting duties. Bescot shed was to provide a regular shunt engine for Great Bridge yard, which had its own small engine shed. The engine returned to Bescot late Saturday afternoon with a return to Great Bridge at 5.00 a.m. on Monday. The Ryecroft shunting engine for Great Bridge also worked the same weekly system as the Bescot engine. The difference with these two shunting engines was the size. Whereas Bescot provided at first a Webb 0-6-0 saddle tank engine with no cab, and later the famous coal engine or its counterpart the coal tank, Ryecroft used its 'Bug'. The 'Bug' is still joked about by retired Ryecroft shed staff. It was to all accounts the most peculiar locomotive ever shedded at Ryecroft. The 'Bug' was one of a class of minute 0-4-0 shunting engines built at Crewe from 1880 under the direction of the chief mechanical engineer of the time, Mr F.W. Webb. With shunting complications on parts of the L&NWR system regarding severe curves and weight restrictions, a small engine was designed with 0-4-0 wheel arrangement and 2ft 6in driving wheels. In fact, it was more or less just a boiler on wheels with a platform or 'footplate' at each end. Unusually, these locomotives had the firebox at one end and the driving controls at the other. A rail was provided at each end for safety. To proceed from each end a person had to walk along a narrow plate clinging to a hand rail placed halfway down the boiler. Despite the complications, these little engines served a very useful purpose, especially within the confines of the large Great Bridge goods yard, adjacent to which were a number of canal interchange basins.

Loco similar to the BUG mentioned in the text which was shedded at Ryecroft in the early 1900s. (John Bucknall Collection)

At the turn of the century a vast amount of Black Country products were transferred from canal boat to railway wagon and vice versa. At Great Bridge, the railway lines leading to these basins dipped down sharply, accompanied by severe curves. This is where this small 'Bug' was a most useful asset. Also, its low weight ratio enabled it to work inches away from the canal. At most times only a few wagons were moved at a time, and in the case of a heavily loaded wagon, only one at a time could be propelled. Whilst shunting alongside the basins, engine crews have been known to fall off into the canal while traversing from one end of the locomotive to another; perhaps the 'Bugs' handrail fastened to the hot boiler had something to do with it! For five days the 'Bug' virtually worked twenty-four hours; the men in those days worked twelve-hour shifts. No coal bunkers were provided on the 'Bug'. Coal was taken as required from a wagon provided. On Saturday shunting took place until late afternoon, then Great Bridge goods yard became still until the first shift started at 6 a.m. the following Monday. This was the time for the 'Bug' to retire to Ryecroft shed for maintenance and boiler washout. The trip of some ten miles usually took about two hours, probably to the embarrassment of its crew who were subjected to remarks from various ranks of railwaymen during its slow progress back to home shed.

Towards the end of the First World War, with canal interchange traffic becoming more demanding, a larger engine was allocated the 'Bug's' duty. The lines were modified within the canal basin confines to enable a Webb 0-6-0 open-cab saddle tank to operate. Any wagons alongside the canal basins could be moved with extra spacer wagons between the engine and any wagons in close proximity to the canal, the extra tractive effort of the Webb tank making this possible. The 'Bug' remained on Ryecroft shed until the grouping of 1923, working one coal wagon at a time up the ramp to the old L&NWR hand-coaling deck which had the water tower overhead. The 'Bug' disappeared from Ryecroft but any mention of the 'Bug' to retired Ryecroft enginemen bought a reminiscent smile to their faces, along with quotes we are unable to print here!

12

Ryecroft Shed 1950–1968

In 1951 Ryecroft steam shed still functioned, its operational conditions little improved since its construction in 1877. Primitive gas lighting illuminated the shed and yard; only the odd lamp was useable outside. Inside fitters relied on their wick 'Aladdin' lamps for illumination at floor level. The depot's water supplies were from the South Staffordshire Waterworks pipeline laid alongside the track from Wychnor Junction to Dudley in 1847, by James Robinson McClean. Drinking and washing water was 'high-tec' filtered for employees use, being percolated over graded pebbles and stones. Toiletry was crude and also equally primitive, consisting of traditional 'pole and bucket' latrines that were emptied weekly and, in summer, were highly unhygienic.

Maintenance conditions were improved in 1935 under LMS control when the chief mechanical engineer, William Stanier, authorised the construction of a mechanical coaling plant and ash recovery unit, and also a larger turntable (60ft) to accommodate the newer and larger locomotives introduced. Similar upgrading of facilities was introduced throughout the LMS system, funded by the Government during the years of Depression. Electricity was introduced to power the new coaling plant, but was not adopted for lighting, the poor illumination of the gas installations in the shed continuing the gloom and semi-darkness, most apparent underneath the locomotives and in the maintenance pits. The archaic set-up had been tolerated during wartime stringency when the shed played a crucial role in the war effort, especially in the transportation of munitions and aircraft workers to factories in the Black Country and Birmingham areas. Even more important was the widespread distribution of coal to the heavy-metal industries producing tanks, bullets, shells and the myriad artefacts of war.

After the cessation of hostilities, it was realised that 1870s technology had to go. Working conditions being of high profile in the new Labour Government's agenda, the shed's insanitary conditions were considered unhealthy and its poor lighting dangerous; it had to change. The establishment of the National Health Service for the prevention, diagnosis and treatment of disease also triggered an in-depth look at Health and Safety in many areas of industry and commerce, including railway installations. In the mid-1950s, Ryecroft

General view across the Cannock line of Ryecroft shed after modernisation, 1952. (Jack Haddock Collection)

shed was 'modernised'. A complete new roof supported by the original shed walls made the interior element proof. Alongside No.1 road, new offices and new facilities, including showers and flush toilets, were incorporated. At long last, efficient electric lighting was installed to improve not only illumination, but safety for fitters and mechanics servicing and repairing locomotives. Electricity also allowed the installation of fixed and mobile power tools, to speed up work schedules and improve productivity, a solution to a need long overdue. The contractors for the modernisation scheme were Edward Ward & Sons Ltd of Derby. It must be assumed that British Railways actively used such contractors to undertake system-wide improvements throughout the country, to drag the railway system from the primitive methods of a Victorian outlook to better reflect the modern era's potential, with larger and more efficient locomotives fitted with labour-saving devices, self-cleaning smoke-boxes, rocking gates, roller bearings and so on, while dieselisation and electrification were being explored in depth as replacements for steam traction.

In 1955 Ryecroft staff received notification that the shed was to be converted to a diesel multiple-unit shed, with a proposed demise of all steam operations within the West Midland area by 1964. Ryecroft had surplus land to the north side of the Mill Lane entrance, and British Railways further proposed and planned a new electric multiple-unit storeage and servicing facility on the proposed site. During Easter 1957, all steam locomotives were transferred from Ryecroft to Bescot shed, some 2 miles away to the south-west. The new diesel multiple units occupied the shed to operate the local passenger services. Work commenced to level and drain nearby land on the other side of Mill Lane for the proposed electric multiple-unit shed, and at the same time work was to be undertaken for all bridges to be raised to allow for overhead 25KV wiring for pantograph pick-up of power. This included the Walsall to Rugeley 'Cannock Branch', which would form a valuable diversionary route to the West Coast mainline at Rugeley

Ryecroft shed minus its roof during the 1951 reconstruction. (*Walsall Observer*)

Trent Valley should this be required, due to maintenance or breakdown on the Stour Valley or Bescot to Bushbury freight lines.

One major problem was the down side Walsall station tunnel running beneath Walsall's very busy Park Street, the site of several large and important retail shops. The only method of gaining clearance was to lower the trackbed which, for the first time, allowed the passage of the Class 8 Stanier 'Pacifics' – a class previously banned from using the route for clearance reasons. A serious lack of foresight in this planning soon became apparent, however, as since the 1849 inception of the South Staffordshire line from Wychnor Junction to Dudley, it closely paralleled the Fordbrook in the Walsall area. The Fordbrook is a tributary of the river Tame which runs through Bescot. As building progress developed around the centre of Walsall, this stream was culverted underneath the town in an area known as the Bridge. The culvert system also went under part of the new Town Hall, constructed in 1902. Insufficient provision was made for storm relief and heavy snowfall thaw. A focal point for flooding was near Butts bridge, as water entered the first culvert. At times of full spate, the water could not be accomodated by the existing construction, and flooded on to the mainline to flow in torrents down the gradient to Walsall station. Within a short time the station could be flooded to platform level, often marooning the signalman in Walsall No.3 signal box located within the tunnel. For such an emergency, the station was provided with a rowing boat to rescue the encumbant signalman. The effect upon an electrified system with its electric points and signal installations could, and should, have been taken into account as the proposed scheme evolved. It wasn't! British Rail requested the Borough Council to consider raising Park Street railway bridge and also buildings on the station down side. If this was feasible, the tunnel roof could be raised to enable passage of electric multiple units and locomotives; to use the Cannock branch, the Brownhills and Sutton lines and gain access to the proposed new electric shed on the old Ryecroft site. Walsall Council refused to participate in such an unpredictable scheme (or gamble), leaving BR 'high and dry', with no other recourse but to abandon the proposed Ryecroft electric multiple-unit shed. The scheme 'sank without trace', defeated by a gentle brook which at times could become a

Modernisation of Ryecroft shed, 1951. Most of the roof has been removed and locos 43410 and 40085 are on view. (Joe Parr)

raging torrent. In 1965 all mechanical signal boxes in the Walsall area were eliminated by the introduction of a new electric power signal box at Pleck Junction.

When Ryecroft shed closed to steam traction in Easter 1957, painting contractors arrived, obviously honouring long-standing contracts to completely paint all service installations. All freight engines went to Bescot 3A, but passenger locomotives were allocated to Mold Junction and other North Wales sheds. Construction engineers immediately began to adapt the depot for diesel multiple-unit traction. The turntable, ash plant; coaling plant and disposal facilities were demolished in order to accommodate up to 12 coach formations, more usually in several smaller units. The ash disposal site was used as a fuelling area with two 5,000-gallon diesel tanks installed. For the first time in Ryecroft's history, female carriage cleaners were employed, and a special luxury toilet was installed complete with showers. However, steam locomotives were still in evidence at Ryecroft until 1964, after which the West Midland area relied solely on 'modern' power. The twice-weekly fuel and stores train arrived from Bescot yard, usually hauled by a Stanier 8F 2-8-0, a type seen at Ryecroft only on rare occasions in the steam era. In winter months and inclement weather, a spare steam locomotive from Bescot was stationed at Ryecroft for the banking of heavy trains on both the Cannock and Water Orton (Sutton Coldfield) lines. A regular sight at Ryecroft was of failed diesel multiple units arriving at the shed behind steam power, and I witnessed this procedure using Stanier 5s and 8Fs, Midland 3 and 4Fs, 'Patriots', 'Jubilees', ex-L&NWR Super Ds, and on one occasion a 'War Department' austerity 2-8-0.

The most severe winter for many years occurred in 1963. A prolonged period of high pressure during January and February brought continuous daytime temperatures below freezing, and nightime readings of 15 degrees below, with bitter winds coming in from the East. Ryecroft drivers and maintenance staff performed miracles to maintain the local passenger service. On visiting the shed confines during the early hours of a freezing cold night one witnessed the sound, sight and smell of rows of diesel multiple units ticking over, in a climate of fog caused by diesel emissions. To start a cold, underfloor horizontal

Rare view of Stanier 'Pacific' 46235 descending towards Mill Lane plus Ryecroft shed on parcels diverted from Nuneaton via Ryecroft to Wolverhampton, then Stafford, 1964. This was only possible because bridge height increases had taken place to prepare for proposed electrification. (Jack Haddock Collection)

Ryecroft again, minus the roof during the reconstruction. This view is seen from the 'Alps' behind the shed, 1951. (Joe Parr)

diesel multiple-unit engine in such extremes of temperature was almost impossible. There was no alternative but to keep engines running in readiness for next-day running, regardless of cost and wear. Sickness rates among staff were considerable and many artisans worked 'overtime' hours well in excess of permitted hours to keep the service going.

An unwelcomed impact on Ryecroft Shed and its local passenger service was a visit by the notorious Dr Beeching on his pruning exercise, hauled in a district engineer's observation car by Bescot Class 2MT 2-6-0 No.46422. I was positioned by North Walsall Junction to record the visit, but at the critical moment was baulked by the torrential

The shed from ground level during reconstruction, 1951. (Joe Parr)

Again taken during reconstruction of shed in 1951, this shows a typical Ryecroft-allocated 2-6-4T loco. (Joe Parr)

rain of a severe thunderstorm, the light available for photography being abysmal – a fitting tribute to this railway vandal. It must be said, however, that deep investigation into loss-making lines had been going on for years by the railway management, Beeching's remit from Government being to wield the axe. By January 1965 the expected closures were announced with all local passenger services withdrawn, leaving only the electrified Walsall to Birmingham service intact, and that was reduced to a once-an-hour service. The service was continuously monitored as a possibility for complete closure, due to competition from buses and private cars.

Ryecroft shed in temporary use as a diesel shed whilst Bescot underwent modernisation, *c.*1966. There is an English Electric type 4 D216 and a multiple unit stabled. (Jack Haddock Collection)

Ryecroft shed in temporary use as a diesel shed whilst Bescot underwent modernisation, *c.*1966. English Electric type 4 D215 is in the yard. (Jack Haddock Collection)

Ryecroft temporarily in use as a diesel repair shed whilst Bescot shed is rebuilt and converted to stable the new power, 1966. (Jack Haddock Collection)

Austerity 9F bringing failed diesel multiple unit into Ryecroft shows the diesel refuelling pad, 1960. (Jack Haddock Collection)

Diesel multiple unit and electric multiple unit used for steam driver familiarisation, seen on shed, *c.*1964. (Jack Haddock Collection)

Ryecroft was in terminal decline by 1965. Monument Lane (Birmingham) closed and Tyseley, the centre of Birmingham diesel multiple-unit operations, was modernised. In 1966 Ryecroft was given a reprieve and temporary lease of life by accommodating the Bescot repair and maintenance unit, complete with the allocation of Bescot's heavy-duty steam crane during the modernisation of Bescot marshalling yard and construction of a new maintenance depot. During 1967 Ryecroft was host to diesel locomotives from Classes 08, 20, 24, 25, 37, 40 and 45. This was Ryecroft's swansong, for in 1968 the shed was closed for good. Rumour got around that the facility might be sold to house and repair heavy goods vehicles during the boom years of this industry, but nothing came of this and in 1970 the structure was demolished. The land was acquired by the local council for recreational purposes and a nature reserve, and by 1998 the land was incorporated as part of the Forest of Mercia. The area's saplings have grown into large willow and birch trees whose growth has been aided by coal, ash and other deposits within the soil from generations of Ryecroft's steam engines.

Above: Rare visit No.1. Ryecroft is host to Scottish-allocated Clan Class loco 72000 *Clan Buchanan*, 1955. (David Spiers)

Left: Rare visit No.2. The Western Regions blue Pullman train is stabled at Ryecroft. It had brought dignitaries from Swansea to Aston Villa's ground for the semi-final of the FA Cup in 1964. (Jack Haddock Collection)

By the millennium only a double-track line remained from Walsall to Ryecroft, splitting there into the Cannock branch and the freight-only line to Water Orton, Derby and Birmingham. The Midland line to Willenhall and Wolverhampton was closed to traffic in 1980, and the South Staffs line to Lichfield in 1984. On the credit side, local passenger services are thriving with diesel multiple-unit operation on the Cannock branch. This route also sees the passage of coal trains to Rugeley B power station, deep mined in Britain's Midland area coalfield or imported via Bristol and other ports.

13

London & North Western Railway Buses, 1913

In order to better promote rail travel to isolated communities, the L&NWR introduced double-decker buses into service in several parts of the country in 1913. One such service was introduced between Brownhills and Hednesford stations, serving Chasetown; Chase Terrace; Heath Hayes and Boney Hay; all mining villages on Cannock Chase. Brownhills station was the hub of the operation, garaging two Milnes Daimler and one Commer Cars vehicles, on land at Brownhills goods yard and canal interchange basin. After the turn of the century Brownhills was a hive of activity, several horse and dray sets distributing parcels and goods throughout the area after transfer from rail.

Two vehicles were in daily use, the third being spare and available to cover maintenance or repair as necessary. The buses were timed to make passenger train connections at the two stations – an early attempt at traffic integration.

Drivers were recruited from the staff at Ryecroft (L&NWR Shed 9) in Walsall, younger men being preferred to their more senior colleagues. The chosen men were Sidney Trubshaw Hayes, Sidney Broughton and William Bate, who were all given instruction in driving and maintenance before commencement of the service on 13 June 1913. All lived adjacent to Ryecroft shed and signed on there, before proceeding to Brownhills by local passenger train (on the cushions) or in the cab of one of the many freight locomotives passing through Brownhills over the old South Staffordshire line. Conductors were recruited from the office staff at Walsall station and Ryecroft shed, their names having gone unrecorded. Takings and receipts were handed in to the chief cash clerk at Brownhills station.

On the opening date of this experimental commuter bus service, crowds gathered at both termini and along the route to witness this innovation. The well-patronised, chain-driven buses with open cabs in immaculate L&NWR livery, surmounted the several steeply inclined roads along the route linking the busy little villages. Children in the street (which at that time would have been liberally spotted with horse droppings!) broke off their play to watch in amazement as the vehicles slowly accelerated from the bus stops leaving a blue haze and a sound signature that soon became part of village

LNWR buses lined up at Brownhills, 1913. These are the vehicles used on the experimental bus service operated by the LNWR between Brownhills and Hednesford to act as passenger feeders to its railway services. Villages served were Chasetown, Chase Terrace and Heath Hayes. The vehicles were requisitioned by the government in 1914 and shipped to France for troop transport duties. (Jack Haddock Collection)

life. Bus stops were closely tied to the village centres, principal shops and public houses. Parcels accommodation was provided over the driver's semi-canopy, which provided only sparse protection against the elements. On the journey over the exposed and windswept Cannock Chase, the drivers resorted to using waterproof rugs, for these were primitive vehicles where creature comforts were few and far between. They were much inferior to the footplate of a Webb coal engine with its cab frontplate and spectacle windows.

The service was successful but was quickly terminated by the outbreak of the First World War, when the vehicles were militarised and converted for war service as troop carriers, offering flexibility and speed. Two of the three drivers volunteered for army service, Bill Bate finding himself in the Royal Army Medical Corps as an ambulance driver working with Ford model T units. Sid Haynes's knowledge of motor vehicles saw him drafted into the Royal Army Service Corps where he drove a variety of early vehicles and remembered seeing ex-railway buses being also used as ambulance and mobile field dressing stations, with another becoming a mobile pigeon loft for pigeons carrying messages from the front line.

On cessation of hostilities, the bus service was not reinstated, Walsall Corporation being granted powers to run services over Cannock Chase, including the pioneering railway bus routes. Sid Broughton returned to Ryecroft after the 1914 withdrawal of the bus service, to work at the shed until his retirement at the age of sixty-five years. He was joined there by Bill Bate when he returned from wartime duties. Sid Haynes, however, on his demobilisation, joined Walsall Corporation, working on its expanding bus fleet as it developed a wide network of routes in the 1920s. He was promoted to motor-bus shed foreman and remained so until his retirement. All three ex-L&NWR bus drivers retired in about 1954, coincidentally all being residents of Webster Road, Walsall. Haynes lived at No.1, Bate at No.77 and Broughton at No.102.

Living on Webster Road since 1929, a couple of hundred yards from Ryecroft shed, I consider myself privileged to know and live with these men and to have collected these notes from the 'Bus' men by conversation or tape recording. This is especially true of Sid Haynes, who I worked with at Birchills bus depot, Walsall, during the Second World War, where I worked as a maintenance engineer and fitter with the Corporation.

Several different location photographs were taken by local businessman Mr Tinsley, who had them made into a series of black and white postcards. These were very popular with visitors or enthusiasts in the area, at the same time giving the 1913 L&NWR service welcome publicity. The excellent originals are typical of the era, where 'slow' films with very fine grain structure preserve much fine detail and definition, and can be enlarged to impressive prints on modern papers.

The buses were chain-driven to the rear axle, with a body-mounted plaque stating, simply, 'Keep Well Oiled' to ensure efficient lubrication. Well-sited lettering was emphatic, 'Speed 12 miles per hour', a ponderous limitation to our generation, but probably very realistic for early and questionable suspensions and braking capabilities available on such early vehicles. The open-topped upper deck was gained by climbing a spiralling staircase from the rear platform to seats of slatted wood. Such an exposed observation area would have been fine in summertime, but not so well patronised in driving rain or exposure to the bitter winds, which were typical of the open and exposed parts of Cannock Chase in winter.

LNWR bus, Brownhills, seen at Brewes Corner, 1913. Named after the cake and confectionery shop shown on the right, the railway station is off to the left. (Jack Haddock Collection)

LNWR bus in Chasetown, 1913. (Jack Haddock Collection)

Selected ambitious young men were chosen to crew the buses, drivers being given training in elementary maintenance and fitting, enabling attention to be given to an ailing or failing vehicle to get it back to base. A simple tool and spares kit would have been carried (spanners, spark plugs, hoses, oil, chain-links and lifting jacks) to overcome any shortcomings in reliability, over the rough potholed and un-metalled roads of the 1910s. Such early road vehicles were never able to approach the reliability records of a steam-hauled railway. Full uniforms and caps were worn – smart looking and a far cry from the typical overalls of the footplate crews. The turnout of both men and machines was purposeful and impressive, as befitted the enterprising new venture. Parcel storage was available on top of the canopied open cab, and large destination boards clearly indicated the routes. The open road beckoned. The 'omnibus' pioneered an industry linking semi-isolated populations, and gave them the mobility to explore and visit towns and villages 20–30 miles away. These pioneer North Western bus crews, perhaps never to achieve fame on a locomotive footplate, became 'Kings of the Road', respected and revered in their daily meanderings over the beautiful and steeply inclined early roadways on the Chase. They were true pioneers of the public service road industry and heralded services allowing both rural and urban populations cheap and timetabled travel which would liberate, stimulate, challenge and encourage travel as we know it today.

14

Known Names, Random Recollections and Ryecroft Enginemen

Known Names of Drivers at Ryecroft Shed

George Warrender
Harry Dodson
Bill Woolley
Ralph Sankey
Jim Jakeman
George Hopley
Jack Fletcher
Bill Weaver
Bob Scrimshaw
Alf Brownjohn
Toffy Everton
Charlie Summers
Charlie Arblaster
Dick Hadiern
Ashley Smith
Dick Worthington
Alf Perks
Bill Booker
Sam Swain
George Jones
Ben Lowbridge
Jack Malaband
Dick Knight
Bill Butler
Harry Cooper
Sid Boughton
Bill Ball (Onlon)
Bill Bate (Butts)
Ernie Priest
Fred Griffiths
Dick Griffiths
Harry Williams
Bill Harrison
Len Allsop
Alf Brittle
Sim Foster
Joe Spooner
Bert Davies
Herb Davies
Arthur Goode
Harold Gould
Arthur Hornblower
Ted Allen
Dan Bennett
Alf Poyner
Sam Malaband
George Shepperson
Arthur Stanley
Frank Fowdrey
Tommy Archer
Joe Brittle
Jim Brittle
George Insley
Sid Hadley
Arthur Hadley
Vic Hateley
Fred Wilson
George Stanley
Tom Hicken
George Hampson
Jim Riley
Sam Frankham
Archie Goodwin
Joe Goodwin
Joe Cooper
Sam Wright
Les Gibbs
Ernle Hartshorn
Frank Poyner
Jack Sanster
Sam Turner
Ernie Pritchett
Dave Condrey
Joe Bradley
Bill Dewson
Fred Dewson
Jim Cooper
Tom Pritchard
Owen Horner
Jack Stanley
Arthur Elsdon
Jim Aston
Sam Cooper
Joe Warltiers
Bill Warltiers
Ted Wells
Frank Plant
Sam Plant
Joe Booker
Alf Wickson
Frank Ash
Sam Brunt
Arthur Hadley
Arthur Thomas
Sid Sturford
George Kesseler

Ernie Jones	Jim Concannon	Bert Smith	Dick Weaver
Ernie Whitehouse	Fred Cooper	Bil Hacket	Bill Millerchip
Jim Mason	Jim Abbotts	George Nutt	Bill Harris
Harry Harris	Jack Steele	Ernle Yates	Garret Dutton
Vic Brewin	Jack Colclough	Walter Poole	Bill Dutton
S. Cooper	Jack Boulton	Bill Perry	Jim Lote
Ben Smith	Fred Jacobs	Tom Kendrick	Harry Stokes
Bill Elmore	Les Foster	Sid Masters	

Some of these men served forty to fifty years at Ryecroft, from L&NWR to LMS and then British Railways control. The Depression years between the two world wars often meant that those in a stable job were not tempted to move on; a regular income was something to be coveted. There were, of course, many other men who joined the railway service, but found that the unsociable and erratic hours worked were not conducive to family or social life. The turnover of staff at Ryecroft, especially after the Second World War, was vast. The availability of well-paid factory jobs with steady shift patterns lured these men away. For the obvious reason that many of their names are not well remembered, they are not included above.

Some of those named above stayed with British Railways beyond the closure date of Ryecroft shed to forge a career on the railways.

Nicknames of Staff at Ryecroft Shed

Drivers

Razzer	Bill Weaver
Toffee	Ted Everton
Slogger	Charles Somers
Hector	Alf Perks
Snooks	Bill Booker
Moaner	Ernie Whitehouser
Pig Shit	Jim Mason
Yum Yum	Harry Harris
Oss Muck	Sam Cooper
Funny Harry	Harry Cooper
Onion	Bill Bate
Banjo	Ernie Priest
Toffee	Harry Williams
Tegsa	Len Allsopp
Mayor of Rushall	Joe Spooner
Brammer	Bert Davis
Sunny	Arthur Goode
Tiny	Ted Allen

Afferonta	George Shepperson
Digger	Arthur Stanley
Ducks	Fred Cooper
Moaner	Jim Brittle
Night Watchman	Arch Hadley
Shitty	George Hampson
Scratcer	Sam Frankhamh
Little Diddler	Arch Goodwin
Poverty Joe	Joe Cooper
Brummie	E. Pritchett
Yarrer	Ernie Yates
Tidlum Buck	Tidman Masters
Steel Chest	Bill Dewson
Piss Corner	Owen Horner
Coddy	Arch Elsdon
Parrot	Bill Waltiers
Bomber	Ted Wells
Fanny	Frank Ash
Iron Arse	Jim Lote

Shed Staff

Honest John	Jack Millett
Skinner	Alf Bickley
Toad	Tom Hawley
Snooks	Bill Booker
Bonnie	Arch Goodwin
Bodger	Arch Atkins

Random Recollections and Ryecroft Enginemen

Fireman Doug Williams's Hardest Day's Work – 1946

Ryecroft was essentially a local passenger and freight shed, its one coveted job being the top-link Class A semi-fitted express freight from Walsall Long Street Goods (Bodley's sidings) to London Camden Town. This important double-trip working was tightly timed, only picking up vans from Bescot and Stechford, these containing important high-value products, trip worked to Stechford from factories and sidings in the Birmingham and Black Country areas. Walsall's speciality was high-class leather products and saddlery, together with finished metal products, many bound for London factories where the components were incorporated into other products. The 'Camden' left Walsall at 8.45 p.m., going mainline to London after its Stechford stop, and was timed to arrive in the capital at 1.30 a.m. On arrival, the crew usually had a meal and were then accommodated

Ryecroft men Sid Middleton and Doug Williams, 1950. (Joe Parr)

at Camden 'barracks' for a night's sleep, having most of the day free before the return trip at about 8.30 p.m. The return train was not regarded as so urgent, going 'slow' line via Northampton, arriving with this Class B train in Walsall at about 4.30 a.m., after some interchange and picking up of wagons en route.

Doug Williams, a young Ryecroft fireman, was preparing his engine on Camden shed for the return trip to Walsall when the duty shed foreman arrived with a problem and a request. Camden at this time had a shortage of top-link firemen. He had a 'Coronation Pacific' due to haul a London–Glasgow express from Euston in about an hour's time; with no fireman available, was he prepared to fire it to Crewe? The return 'Walsall' was not so urgent and could wait until a junior grade fireman could be allocated to the easier duty. This chance of a lifetime to fire a 'Coronation Pacific' was quickly seized. Obviously a tough job, but welcome if only for the experience. Firing the huge 50sq. ft firebox would be a challenge; his temporary mate would obviously give him a few tips. Doug knew of the 'Pacific's' reputation for being totally in control of its work, its wide and efficient grate responding to a wide variety of firing techniques. It would obviously not be 'a little and often' that he was used to, but a real test of stamina, this huge loco having a fire-grate you could 'hold a party in'. At the end of the war, overnight Glasgow and Perth trains had some sleeper accommodation included, so a load anywhere between 500 and 600 tons was normal in 'limited' timings.

Doug certainly did not have much time to adapt and did well to keep up steam, despite the new techniques required by such a huge and powerful locomotive. He later admitted that it had been the toughest firing turn he had ever experienced, and quickly learned that mainline express work certainly deserved the larger pay packet. His big Stanier was indeed a thoroughbred and a pleasure to fire. A few days later, a note of thanks was passed on to the Ryecroft shed master from the hierarchy at Crewe, commending Doug Williams for his volunteered effort and unexpected stint with the shovel. Returning home from Crewe 'on the cushions', he could relax and relive his miles on the footplate of a dream machine. He little realised that by the early 1960s fully fitted Crewe- and Carlisle-bound freights would be allocated regularly to the class, as diesels and electrics took over their Class 1 duties. He would certainly have welcomed one of these 'Big Uns' for the Walsall–London job. It would have murdered the 'Camdens'.

Vic Hately, Ryecroft Marathon Walker

The official appreciation of Doug William's efforts was not often given, as Ryecroft fireman Vic Hately was to find out. On a Christmas Eve just before the Second World War, the last local passenger train from Walsall to Derby was in the station awaiting departure time when its fireman was taken ill. Vic happened to be on Walsall Station at the time and was asked to undertake the journey to Derby. He accepted (in reality he had no choice), and by the time he arrived at the county town it was early Christmas morning and he was to receive a very unwelcome Christmas box.

He soon learned there was no return train to Walsall and the authorities had not made any special provision for his return to Ryecroft. No one was available to help or advise, so he went to one of the station's signal boxes with his problem. In this emergency a very unofficial solution was found. A very late train was due, bound for sleeping Birmingham, and was held while Vic explained his plight to the footplate crew, who agreed to make an unofficial stop in the wilds at Wychnor Junction, midway between Burton and Tamworth, at least getting Vic part of the way home but leaving him with a walk of about 15 miles. The most direct route seemed to be to follow the track through Lichfield. So on a cold night in mid-winter, Vic dropped off the footplate, thanked the crew and started his long walk as the train accelerated away over the Trent, climbing towards Tamworth. Being young and fit he set a good pace, eventually getting to Ryecroft some four hours later. On arrival he was confronted by a Scrooge-like foreman quoting rules and regulations and asking why he had walked the rails instead of following the roads. His verbal Christmas present was in total contrast to his fellow footplate-men who had helped when officialdom did not want to know, all at home snoring and probably well filled with Christmas cheer.

Fred Haywood

Fred Haywood was born in Francis Street in the Birchills district of Walsall. He had four brothers and three sisters. His father was, for many years, a professional footballer with Crewe Alexandra and West Bromwich Albion. On his retirement from football, he worked at the Walsall Lock & Cart Gear Co. in Neale Street, just off Hollyhedge Lane in Walsall. He was generally known by his nickname of 'Nutty', his son Fred continuing as 'Nutty' after his father's death. Fred inherited his father's football skills of vision, fine ball control and being a superb 'team' player.

Life in the Birchills at that time, with its close-packed Victorian housing, was hard, the family being brought up to be socialist minded. Fred attended the Wolverhampton Road School from the age of five until he was fourteen. He was a pupil of well above average intelligence and potential, and was asked by his headmaster to sit the Grammar School

Ryecroft disposal road with Fred Haywood on loco 44115, 1955. (Jack Haddock Collection)

Fred Haywood preparing Class 4 tank loco 42586 for duty, 1954. (Joe Parr)

entrance examination. His record was impressive. In each of his year groups most teachers gave him top marks for his school work, mathematics being his best and favourite subject. Due to lack of family finances, when a Grammar School place had to be paid for, his potential was perhaps never realised as he had to leave school at fourteen to bring in an extra wage to help support the large family. The headmaster at Wolverhampton Road was a Mr Le Bon, a stern but fair man who would not tolerate misbehaviour, wasted time or lack of concentration. Discipline and encouragement of self-discipline was very evident in the running of the school, which always had a reputation for producing able and self-confident scholars coming from working-class families. This background and environment of a solid work ethic within the school, gave Fred the basis, along with support from his headteacher, to become a reliable and efficient workman when accepted by the London, Midland & Scottish Railway.

He started work at Ryecroft in 1924 on sweeping up and 'knocking up' duties, the first step on the ladder at any loco shed. He was allocated to the Coalpool village and Rushall areas, which meant regularly passing Ryecroft cemetary in the middle of the night in all weathers, to ensure train crews reported for duty on time. Not easily put off, and self-confident, Fred soon recognised the white shirted apparitions appearing eerily in the hedgerows, with chains and moans, to be Ryecroft staff out to test the youngster's metal, an initiation every 'knocker up' had to endure as part of the high jinx antics typical of the shed. Fred was made of better stuff than some of the youngsters, who would qualify as Olympic runners judging by the speed they generated 'legging it' from such encounters. Even at an early age, new recruits soon got into the spirit of Ryecroft. Fred remembered a call-up lad known as 'Moke' Cook, who developed a habit of borrowing a donkey from a field adjacent to the shed to act as transport during his night duty With the absence of any management at night, he always brought the animal back into the shed to give it some scraps and a drink of water amongst the rows of locomotives, before returning it to its field and freedom. Whether its owner ever thought the animal was a little tired during the day, and prone to drop to sleep, will never be known. It was most convenient that the donkey could not talk.

Fred was later offered a job as fitter's mate, with a view to becoming a qualified fitter, but the economic climate of the 1920s, particularly regarding the manpower situation, was to make life difficult for Fred and many others at Ryecroft shed. The problem was compounded in that during the First World War extra men had been taken on to replace young railwaymen who had volunteered for active service in the forces. With the slump, which lasted from the 1920s almost until the outbreak of the Second World War, work was both difficult to obtain and keep at Ryecroft. The LMS was in a dilemma. With falling amounts of traffic and consequent loss of revenue, it wanted to shed manpower without having the embarrassment of sacking them. The solution was staff flexibility, as men were moved from low-grade jobs in all departments to fill vacancies occurring in other areas of the country. This could be locally or hundreds of miles away, with a promised return to Ryecroft as and when trade picked up and need occurred. This ploy suited the company, but could make life almost impossible for the men, especially if they were married with young families or had elderly parents to support. Sometimes lodging away could take nearly two thirds of an already poor income and with no prospect of dole money, owing to the Government rules at the time, most railwaymen chose to tolerate the inconvenience and hardship of these dubious jobs at often isolated outposts on the railway system, until better times.

One day in 1932, after gaining much experience and ready to become a fully qualified fitter, the shed superintendent informed Fred that he had to report to a small North Wales station called Pagewell and Buckly, where he would have to accept demotion and a cut in pay on becoming a station porter. Having just got married and his wife expecting their first child, Fred had no option but to leave Walsall, or face the sack. He was living with his in-laws while awaiting a council house. If he put in his notice there was no prospect of work of any kind locally during the 1930s Depression years. Fred took the post and got lodgings in a row of terraced railway cottages, with a railway family providing this facility at a reasonable rate. This also served at the same time to supplement their own income. One bright aspect in his enforced transfer was the travel-pass system which enabled Fred's wife to occasionally visit him, or he to return to Walsall. Fred was fortunate his new posting was transport feasible.

Fireman John Ballard was not so fortunate. He found himself posted to Thurso in Scotland as a porter, finding it impossibly distant. He was unable to use his free passes as the whole of his time available for leave would be taken up by a time-consuming return journey. Because of his two-year exile and picking up a bit of the strong Scottish accent, he was immediately nicknamed 'Jock' on his return to Ryecroft.

Fred eventually managed to return from portering in North Wales to go cleaning at Saltley Shed, Birmingham, a convoluted experience which promotion and career-wise left him no further advanced, but at least he could now live at home. To save waiting for trains between Walsall and Birmingham, he bought a bicycle. Fred was fortunate to be one of a group of cleaners at Saltley who were deputed to work for a week or two for an unusual assignment at the Castle Bromwich Industries Fair. This was to clean and maintain the LMS's most famous locomotive, No.6100 *Royal Scot*, which had just returned from a long exhibition tour in the United States in 1933. The locomotive was a centrepiece attraction of the show. Saltlely was tolerable, but Fred still craved for a return to Ryecroft and to rent a house for his wife and daughter. At Saltley he did progress to become a fireman, and eventually returned to Ryecroft in 1934 when a situation became available. Having, like many other staff at Walsall, been compulsorily transferred to 'foreign' parts of the LMS empire, it was no surprise that Fred and virtually all the footplate and artisan staff at Walsall became active members of either ASLEF or the NUR, hoping that union support might improve conditions of service and rates of pay for their future years of railway service. Many became devout socialists and supported the Labour Party.

During the uneasy years of the late 1930s, the men of Ryecroft had survived and earned a slightly better wage than many industrial workers, but always had problems with management. However, the shed superintendent, union officials and men somehow worked together in reasonable harmony, when compared with other local sheds. A sense of humour, practical jokes and a jovial comradeship was a necessity in Ryecroft life, and the atmosphere at the shed was vibrant, no one knowing or expecting the next lightning bolt or on whom it might fall. Visiting crews always referred to 3C as a 'happy shed'.

Almost all Ryecroft men managed to get houses within a mile's radius of the shed, mainly in the Ryecroft, Butts and North Walsall districts of the borough. A family spirit

Ryecroft steam driver's diesel multiple unit training near Rugeley, 1956. Driver Fred Haywood is on the extreme right instructing staff on new diesel units. (Jack Haddock Collection)

was strong at Ryecroft, the shed with about 300 employees having very fine sporting traditions, producing very good football and cricket teams that performed well in inter-shed competitions within the LMS, and where the football talent of the Haywood family continued to flourish.

Fred Haywood was offered a transfer to Crewe North Shed (5A) for mainline duties and promotional prospects. This was management inspired, as there had been a close relationship between LMS Crewe and Crewe Alexandra, where it was hoped Fred might continue his football on a semi-professional basis in the football league, as did his father. However, this was not to be as his wife refused to move from her native Walsall. Fred stayed at Ryecroft until the shed's closure to steam locomotives in 1957, and then transferred to nearby Bescot until his retirement.

Fred was a very popular workmate, easy going and respected by staff and management alike. As stated before, he was a very keen union man and was known by all at the shed as the '101 per cent man'. He was totally dedicated, always doing his best and a quiet 'Good Samaritan', offering sound advice and practical help as and when required. A fountain of good sense and reliability, with an easy going manner, he was good company and a trusted friend to many of his workmates in their time of need. He always considered that to drive a locomotive was a challenge, a sublime mutual partnership between man and machine, working in total harmony – yet another Ryecroft thoroughbred, whose mettle had been sorely tried in adversity and had emerged a triumphant spirit.

Freddie Keay

Freddie Keay was the smallest driver at Ryecroft Shed, being only 5ft 4in tall and of small build. Starting work in 1913, he was 'called-up' for the army in 1916, spending two years in France and two years after the 1918 cessation of hostilities in Germany with the Army of Occupation, before returning to Ryecroft duties in 1920.

Just before joining the army, while unloading wagon loads of coal to build up an emergency coal stack for winter operations close to the busy Cannock line, over the noise and hiss of the depot's steam engines and a few expletives and oaths as others unloaded the wagons for 6*d* a ton, a strange noise was heard in the sky above. The surprised Ryecroft men looked up to see their first aeroplane misfiring, spluttering and obviously in difficulty. Believed to be one of the first planes to fly over Walsall, the pilot was using the railway tracks and towns to help in navigation over his cross-country route, and was fighting to keep his plane airborne. He was in such trouble, however, that he was evidently intent on an emergency landing on a small grass field between Brewer Street and the Cannock line. Fred and his mates watched in horror as the engine failed totally at slow speed. The flimsy flying machine tried to circle to maintain airspeed but then spun earthwards to crash in the back garden of a cottage. The railwaymen ran to the site of the accident and freed the pilot from the wreckage. He had a broken leg but, sadly, his stricken machine had fallen on an elderly lady nursing a baby in her arms, and both were killed instantly. The army officer pilot was placed on a cart to be taken to Walsall Cottage hospital, but by this time a huge crowd had assembled to witness the tragic event. Fred remained calm, having witnessed many casualties in his war service.

On return from overseas, he resumed duties at Ryecroft as a cleaner, eventually graduating to become a fireman. Because of the 1923 grouping and formation of the LMS, the Midland Railway's shed at New Mills, Pleck, was closed in 1925, and its men were dispersed for further duty at Ryecroft and other places. Amongst them was their senior driver, Dick Hodean. At about the same time Walsall Permanent Way Department had been re-organised so that it took responsibility for maintaining the ex-Midland tracks from Wychnor Junction to Birmingham and as far as Bristol and Avonmouth docks. The engineer was resident at the Springfields Permanent Way Depot situated close to the Pleck Gas Works, where a small shed housed his inspection saloon. A regular Ryecroft engine crew were allocated to this duty, together with a L&NWR Jumbo with its cab-side nameplate reading 'Engineer Walsall'.

One of Fred's first firing turns was on this locomotive. Freddie Keay was firing for Dick Hodean on the day of the Charfield railway disaster, tragically with loss of life, as wooden-bodied, gas-lit Midland coaches caught fire on impact. Quickly transporting the engineer to the site of the accident, the crew picked up as close to the wreckage as possible, Fred being told by his driver to keep his fire low to conserve coal, as it would be some time before a return to Walsall. From the footplate all they could do was witness and contemplate the carnage and destruction of the burnt-out wreckage which met their eyes.

After some eight hours at the scene, all their tea and snap had been consumed. Some time later a Salvation Army mobile canteen was set up and proceeded to offer refreshment to Police, Firemen and exhausted rescue workers. The loco crew had obviously been

Midland Railway loco 157 arriving on shed at Ryecroft, 1934. This was the loco used by the permanent way engineer and would have been driven by Freddie Keay as related in the text. (John Bucknall collection)

forgotten and Fred, who by this time was getting desperate for a drink, collected his tea can and descended to the track with a view to obtaining refreshment. He was ordered back to the footplate by his driver, a hard 'rules' man, who insisted that the engineer who was still supervising operations, would have to give the permission. In reality it was a continuation of the 'superiority' feud practised by Midland men having to accept work at an L&NWR shed, and maintaining the long-standing antagonism going back over many years. Eventually the Army arrived at the engine with tea and sandwiches, instructed by the engineer. It was some thirty-six hours before the engineer decided to return to Walsall, the locomotive fortunately being parked adjacent to a water column for replenishment of the tender. Their thankless duty at Charfield almost accounted for two whole days in total, but time off was allowed before their next duty. Fred was very pleased with his next pay packet, as overtime was generally scarce in the 1920s, taking a good 'ribbing' by enquiries as to when the wheelbarrow would be returned after taking his wages home.

Like others at Ryecroft, Fred sometimes broke or bent the rules appertaining to railway routine. Fred was living in Spout Lane, Caldmore, and one day decided on a shortcut to his home by walking the tracks from Ryecroft to Walsall station's platform 5, from there going through the 'Back Yard' coal sidings to nearby Bradford Place and a No.3 bus. Emerging from Park Street tunnel with time to spare, he encountered the senior movements inspector on the northern extremity of platform 5. The inspector, who was over 6ft tall, towered above the considerably smaller frame of Fred. 'I believe you are off duty Keay', he said. Fred, of course, agreed. 'Then you will please accompany me to Ryecroft shed', said the inspector. With nothing else said the young man feared the worst, a probable visit to the shed superintendent's office to see the 'Gaffer', Mr Waddington, renowned for his obsession with discipline. Slowly, Fred's journey was retraced along the busy track, trains passing every few minutes. Fred was escorted on to the shed, through lines of locomotives and shed cleaners, most curious about what the miscreant had been up to. To his utmost surprise the chief's office was passed as the pair headed for the shed's official entrance gate in Mill Lane. Duly opening the creaking structure, the inspector remarked, 'Fireman, that is the way in or out of Ryecroft shed, walking along the tracks can be dangerous, so please abide by the company's rules and you will keep out of the traffic'. With that mild admonition, the inspector retired to the shed. Fred, now very late, set out once more for home, reflecting on his good fortune after an incident which could have seen him suspended from duty or possible dismissal.

After this incident Fred became a driver, almost invariably wearing a flat cap instead of the company issue and having no further trouble until his retirement. From the 1957 withdrawal of steam traction from the shed, he worked on the replacement diesel multiple units on local passenger services in the area.

After his departure from the railway, at the age of sixty-five, he kept in close contact with his former colleagues by becoming a doorman at the new Pleck Railway Men's Club. Fred passed away in 1969 on his way to the club on 11 November, at around the time of the Armistice Service.

George Cauldicott

George Cauldicott started at Ryecroft as a call-up lad and cleaner in the late 1920s. After the long drawn-out process of promotion up the 'ladder', he became a driver. His career at this point enabled him to get experience in the varied links, but he enjoyed all aspects of his work, especially working on heavy freight, usually with a 'Super D'. On arrival at Ryecroft one day, just about to prepare his mount for its rostered duty, George was called into the office for an interview. He was told that there was a need for a driver to work at Hednesford. If accepted, this would be regular work, not shift work, and would be nominally in the shunting link, but offering a variable routine and would need special training at Hednesford.

George knew the Hednesford yards well. In reality, although on a rising approach from Rugeley to Hednesford Town, the yard could be considered as the centre of a huge, imaginary household saucer, with many collieries at higher level on the run pouring coal into the massive and complex sidings on either side of the mainline. Sorting was then carried out before assembly into trains for dispatch to Walsall's Bescot yard. From here the coal would be distributed countrywide, but especially to the highly industrialised West Midlands. With its huge concentration of factories, manufacturers, chemical plants and iron and steel production facilities, the area as a whole was known as the 'Black Country'. With the enormous movements of loaded coal and empty pit-bound wagons, a daytime shunting engine was always on duty from early morning to evening. The sidings extended from west of Hednesford station along the length of Station Road to the Rawnsley Road, about half a mile in length, and for this duty Ryecroft provided a L&NWR-derived 0-8-0 ('Super D') with a resident driver. The fact that a considerable wagon repair depot was established on the Cannock side of Hednesford station is testament to the enormous numbers of empty and full wagons passing through the yard on a daily basis. The facility could cope with anything from light repairs to total heavy rebuilding of wagons after considerable normal 'wear and tear' or accident.

As there were many collieries flooding coal into the busy yards, shunting movements were intense and often complex, the railway control deeming it wise to appoint a regular shunting driver to familiarise himself with every aspect of operation at this hub yard. George Cauldicott was appointed to the post, but other Ryecroft men had to be familiar with the job to act as relief, as the hours of almost round the clock activity far exceeded the normal working hours of George's shift. Daily traffic was beyond the capacity of a single-shunt engine, so almost any passing goods or mineral train was diagrammed to attach and detach wagons and assist in wagon shunting movements in both up and down directions. Most of these mineral trains were worked by Bescot men, who, after shunting and train formation, worked trains across the Norton Branch to Norton Junction, where further marshalling took place, before continuing to Bescot and Black Country destinations. George Cauldicott's specialist knowledge was enhanced by training on the industrial lines serving local collieries; this was because some colliery company lines were maintained by the LMS and later British Railways permanent way engineers. These lines were visited by the Walsall engineer's saloon for annual inspections, the motive power normally being a Ryecroft 2P 4-4-0, with George taking over as footplate supremo from the regular engineer's driver. The visits always coincided with George's 6 a.m. to 2 p.m. shift allocation. Resident relief drivers replaced him for the less important 2 p.m. to 10 p.m. shift. George signed on daily at Ryecroft at 5 a.m. to take his 'Super D' light engine to Hednesford for the complex, demanding and intense activity.

The 'D' allocated to the shunt was normally one which had run a high mileage and was getting towards its next shopping at Crewe, its mainline haulage work being undertaken by a sister engine in better general mechanical condition. The tender on the shunt engine was always fully loaded on leaving Ryecroft for the day's duty and if running short during the afternoon shift, would be replaced by another 0-8-0 ferried out from Ryecroft as replacement, the substituted loco returning home. A fill-in turn between heavy shunting allowed George's engine to travel down to Brereton Colliery Sidings, Rugeley, to lift a loaded train up to Hednesford after delivering a raft of empties.

George Cauldicott was uniquely summoned from bed every morning by the call-up boy loudly beating a huge brass gong at the bottom of George's stairs. George retired when Ryecroft shed closed for steam operations in 1957, with responsibility for the Hednesford shunt then falling to Bescot shed.

George Hall – A Ryecroft Artisan

In any depot the men on the footplate were always the focus of attention, and rightly so. Their trials and tribulations were admired and penned by many reporters, including this volume. Even a life on the footplate was not always what it could have been, but there were other vital jobs necessary to running a fleet of steam locomotives, which were of much lower esteem and offering much poorer remuneration. Less glamorous and less publicised was the roll of the shed's 'artisan' class, here typified by another of Ryecroft's labourers, George Hall. These were often men with less than perfect vision, which immediately barred them from a footplate career, or men who never did aspire to the throne being quite contented with any regular job available, especially in hard times and the Depression, where a regular, if limited, income was appreciated in a time and era before the establishment of the protective net of a welfare state.

A labourer's lot was characterised by hard work and, without saying, long hours. Up until 1936 Ryecroft had no mechanised coaling plant, this operation being a manual transfer from truck or piled coal stock to tender, a tough physical and continuous job which bordered on slave labour. Likewise, labourers on the disposal pits had to rake out the red-hot grates and ash pans, and remove clinker from locomotive fireboxes in whatever conditions the weather could throw at them – red-hot summer's heat, bitter, penetrating cold gale-force winds, thunder storms or continuous torrential rain. Cleaning the char from a well-filled smoke-box in a blustery wind, which blew ash into watering eyes and susceptible lungs, was accepted with stoicism and little complaint. This job was considered more acceptable than manhandling the buckets of human excrement from primitive pole and bucket latrines, to be buried in a pre-dug hole, and all for the princely sum of 3*d* (1.25p in today's terms) per hour, by a less than generous railway company. Another necessity of almost all loco sheds was George Hall's speciality. He was appointed as the shed's rat catcher – no fancy names for the position in those days, no softening of edges by adoption of the title 'Rodent Operative' or some similar modern euphemism to blur and flatter life's realities, as is so often attempted today.

Rats thrived in abundance within the confines of Ryecroft due to the close proximity of the nearby Fordbrook, whose banks are still today treated with Warfarin as a means of pest control. The shed's mess room, with its large heating stove, was always an attraction by virtue of the supply of stale sandwiches left by hard-worked operatives and footplate crews, who had to exit quickly or had little time to eat. George Hall operated a number of box-type traps around the shed which caught rodents alive. One method of elimination was to confine them in the depot's turntable pit and then call in some terrier dogs. George, however, had a round-the-clock competitor in Clara the cat, a long-time resident of the shed, being well cared for and fed scraps brought from home by many of the 300-strong workforce. She would regularly kill a rat and bring it for presentation before the mess room fire while the men were eating their snap, the rat's exit from the world often being cremation in a locomotive firebox.

George Hall and his fellow shed labourers were the lowest paid men on Ryecroft's books, and if they could find extra work outside their jobs they did, especially during the Depression years of the 1930s. One day George surprised and amused the Ryecroft workforce by writing out an application for the nationally advertised post of public hangman for the Crown. He was apparently shortlisted for the job and brought the necessary confirmation papers to show his mates, but was later informed that the vacancy for this most distressing of occupations had been filled. He had retired by the time the old North-light L&NWR shed roof had been rebuilt when the steam shed was modernised in 1952. The depot closed to steam operations in 1957, being used to stable diesel multiple units until 1965, before being demolished in 1970. Left to the reclaiming energies of nature, birch and other wind-planted saplings have become established on the site. Descendents of Ryecrofts rodents are still sought and eagerly hunted by Kestrels, which nest in nearby trees and under the shelter of Mill Lane bridge. Ryecroft is now largely a wildlife sanctuary within the town, with a thriving population of urban foxes – you could say they are George Hall's natural successors as rodent exterminators on the old 3C shed site.

Harry Harris

Harry Harris commenced his railway service at Ryecroft shed, Walsall, in 1924. Harry's early childhood life was unhappy and grim. He was an orphan who spent his early days in foster care until the age of ten. The next eight years of his life were spent within the confines of the Princess Alice orphanage at New Oscott, Birmingham. He then acquired living accomodation with a distant relative at Aston, Birmingham, his first employment being as a cleaner at Aston shed, transferring to Ryecroft after two years, still as a cleaner. He passed through the promotion grades to become fireman, driver and diesel multiple-unit driver until Ryecroft closed in 1965.

Harry married in 1928 and he and his wife had two children, his family being the delight of his life. He became a well-respected member of the Ryecroft fraternity, a strong socialist in politics with a strong willingness to help others with advice and more practical help. Harry Harris had a close affinity with shedmate Sid Hadley. Sid worked the last diesel multiple-unit service from Birmingham New Street to Rugeley in January 1965, his mate driving for the returning Rugeley to Birmingham journey. Harry appreciated the improved conditions and the establishment of the welfare state and health service, and the better prospects and general prosperity during his later life. He had a keen interest in his home town and its history, and recorded his memories of his orphanage years; these tapes are now adding to the archive information filed in the Walsall Local History Centre. Listening to the tapes certainly demonstrates the massive social change in welfare and living conditions, improved housing and prosperity achieved since 1945 and the cessation of hostilities. Both Harry and Sid had unblemished records over their many years of Ryecroft service, becoming great role models of skill, experience and character that many young Ryecroft recruits aspired to follow during the development of their railway careers. In adversity or difficulty, Ryecroft closed ranks, its mutual concern and self-help being legendary.

Hector Perks

Hector Perks started work at Ryecroft in L&NWR days, graduating from cleaner to driver and retiring in 1954. He lived in an old block of terraced houses at the corner of Mill Street and Brewer Street, only a couple of hundred yards from the loco shed. Reputedly, he was never late for work, gave good service to the company and retired with an unblemished record of safety and reliability. Living so near to the shed, any emergency for a driver would find the 'call lad' knocking on his door, when he was off duty if the stand-by link men were occupied. If absent from home, then other drivers living near the shed and not on duty would be called out.

An amusing footplate incident involving Hector was recalled by driver Fred Haywood. It took place on a local passenger train working between Stafford and Wellington just a short time after the end of the Second World War. Six years of blackout conditions had been in force during hostilities, when the cabs of tender engines had to be covered by sheets, and side windows on tank engines blacked out to minimise glare from an open firebox, lights which might be seen by hostile enemy aircraft at night. Signals were, likewise, fitted with dimmed reflectors and station lights subdued, which made footplate life difficult, just as cars with masked headlights made night driving on the highways a veritable lottery.

Late one evening Hector Perks and Fred Haywood were heading west and approaching Wellington, the weather conditions throwing up areas of patchy mist from the small streams and ponds adjacent to the railway. Running slowly in readiness for the Donnington stop, Hector suddenly made an emergency brake application which took Fred by surprise and almost pinned him against the firebox. 'What are you doing?', exclaimed the fireman, as he tried to retrieve his posture, blowing on his hands. 'I've got a red on', replied Hector. Fred climbed down from the footplate into the light mist to see a bright red light ahead that had no relationship to any known signal. Fred regained the footplate to inform his driver to proceed with caution and ease the train forward to Donnington station. As the locomotive gained speed, under very light steam, the signal box ahead stood firmly sentinel in the billowing mist, the brakes were applied and Fred retired to the box for an explanation of the mysterious red light. This was still highly visible and now obviously some distance away. Fred was informed that the Air Ministry had sanctioned a new aircraft warning light on the top of the Wrekin, a shapely tree-covered volcanic plug rising 1,334ft above the Shropshire plain. The original light had been removed at the outbreak of hostilities with Germany in September 1939, to prevent it being used as a navigational aid. This was the first night that the guiding beacon had been re-energised. Fred once again hauled on the grab rails to achieve footplate height and a broad grin on his face suggested that Hector had better get his eyes tested, but accepted the fact that the swirling misty conditions were the cause of Hector Perk's dilemma. This was yet another occasion which sparked off a great deal of leg-pulling among his colleagues at Ryecroft as the story got around.

The possibility of a few drivers suddenly acquiring eye-patches in readiness for a chance encounter with Hector could not be ruled out, or the fact mentioned that H. Perks had found a 'red light' area in rural Shropshire.

Horner's Corner

Life at Ryecroft shed during the 1930s could be described as happy, despite the prevailing Depression. The men at Ryecroft were lucky to have regular, if demanding, jobs. The reason for the spirit of comradeship at the shed was the result of many Ryecroft men serving in the forces during the First World War. To relieve the monotonous routine of shift work and the bad working conditions, practical jokes and humour were the order of the day. Most of the staff had a nickname that, once bestowed on an individual, lasted them for the remainder of their working life.

Owen Horner started his local railway career with the Midland Railway as a cleaner at the New Mills shed, Pleck. He graduated to fireman prior to the 1923 grouping of railways. The outcome of this grouping in the Walsall area was to close the Midland shed and transfer locomotives and staff to Saltley, Bescot and Ryecroft sheds. This transfer took place in 1925 and Owen Horner was to report to Ryecroft. It was a number of years before Owen graduated to driver, owing to surplus manpower on the railway with the subsequent Depression between the two world wars. It was in the mid-1930s that he began to gain driving experience on local passenger trains. At the first opportunity he applied to learn the roads to Lancashire and the North Wales seaside resorts. These trips were a good means of procuring extra money that was so useful, particularly during the Depression. He did his best to learn as many roads as possible in a short time. This haste was to lead to a serious mistake on one of his first Blackpool excursions. The trip in question was a 'special', consisting mainly of school children. It was a twelve-coach train and was hauled by one of the two new 5xP 'Jubilee' class locomotives allocated to Ryecroft shed, No.5603 'Solomom Islands'. Perhaps the thrill and responsibility of working one of these new Stanier locomotives for the first time was the cause of Owen's momentary lapse of concentration. A signal box was situated a few miles on the down side of Weaver Junction, at Hartford. When passing Hartford, down expresses were required to whistle a code to inform the Weaver Junction signalman which route the train was going to take, mainline to the North or branch to Runcorn and Liverpool.

Owen, for some unknown reason, completely forgot to whistle at Hartford. He approached Weaver Junction at considerable speed, only to see his road was signalled to Liverpool instead of Preston and Blackpool. Owen Horner had reached the point of no return. He didn't know the road to Liverpool and did the only thing possible, stopping in section at the first signal box. He reported his mistake to the signalman, who was not exactly pleased with this interruption to his routine and margins, not to mention the detailed reports which would need to be filled out later. There was no alternative but to hold the special until a pilot (another man who did know the road) arrived and, as a consequence, the down Liverpool line was blocked for some time. The area control worked very fast and decided to route the special via Southport to meet the North West mainline again at Preston. On arrival at Preston, the pilot left Owen Horner to make his way to Blackpool, where the special's arrival was about two hours late. The evening return was accomplished with Owen Horner taking extra care with the numerous whistling codes at the many junctions en route. Owen submitted his report after arrival at Ryecroft shed, and was duly instructed to visit the superintendant at Bescot shed the following day. It was not a pleasant interview. Owen finished up with one week's suspension of duty without pay, and was also put back into the mundane shunting links with no excursion work for some time.

An event like this is not easily forgotten by railwaymen. In the case of the Ryecroft men it became an indelible memory. Once you made a mistake or practised jokes on your fellow men, it was remembered for a long time, not with malice but with a sense of humour. The victims took it in their stride, knowing deep down that their fellow men understood and had some sympathy. After all, this was not an isolated case as others also made mistakes. This one event, however, of a Ryecroft excursion taking the wrong road, became notorious between Walsall and the Cheshire and Lancashire mainlines. No one at Ryecroft knows who gave Weaver Junction the title of 'Horner's Corner' after this episode, but it is a fact that even today, fifty years later, many local and West Coast mainline railwaymen still call Weaver Junction 'Horner's Corner'. Anyone reading this true story of Ryecroft life may think that a mistake like the one Owen Horner made would seriously

hinder his progress. Indeed not, for Owen gradually made his way to Ryecroft's top-links, gaining experience on the way. With the advent of the Second World War and the extra demand for railwaymen, Owen applied for a transfer to Crewe North shed. He was granted a move that was to prove permanent, and by the end of the war he was a top-link driver with knowledge of the West Coast mainline between London and Glasgow, and also to Perth. He had a clean record until his retirement and had obviously paid special attention to whistle codes. Owen must have passed Weaver Junction many times whilst at Crewe and knew of the term 'Horner's Corner', but I doubt if he knew that name would still be known today. Owen has now passed on and with him memories of railway life before the Second World War.

Jack Boulton's Progression to Driver at Ryecroft Shed

Step 1	5 callers up	Work round on turns
Juniors		6.00 a.m. – 2.00 p.m.
		2.00 p.m. – 10.00 p.m.
		3 on night duty
		10.00 a.m. – 6.00 p.m.
	Ryecroft District	
		12.00 midnight – 8.00 p.m.
	Butts District	
		12.00 midnight – 8.00 p.m.
	Leamore District	

Right: Standard 9F Class loco 92163 on Ryecroft diesel shed awaiting transfer after closure of Bushbury shed, Wolverhampton, in 1964, with driver Jack Boulton and fireman Harry Bird. (Jack Haddock Collection)

Opposite: Locos on loan for Bank Holiday seaside specials arriving on Ryecroft disposal line, 1955. (Jack Haddock Collection)

Step 2

After two or three years calling up the next step was tubeplate cleaning, i.e. entering the firebox to remove clinker that builds up on the ends of the element tubes and on the roofing stays, replacing burnt firebars and so on in preparation for the boilersmith to do his periodical examination, and entering the water tanks to remove any debris and scale that accumulates around the water feed to the injectors.

Step 3

Engine Cleaning - there were three shifts of cleaners (6.00 a.m. – 2.00 p.m., 2.00 p.m. – 10.00 p.m., 10.00 p.m. – 6.00 a.m.), usually about ten on each shift. The senior men were available for any firing duty as required – firing duties were given on seniority basis. The junior men could be utilised on labouring duties or any other duties as required, i.e. coaling engines, fitters mates, ashpan raking etc. – in general, any eventuality around the clock. When a cleaner attained 313 firing turns, his basic pay went up to 57*s* per week; a further 313 turns up to 63*s*; another 313 turns 72*s* per week.

Step 4

Registered fireman - as a registered fireman he would first be put on shunting duties, shed turning and so on, eventually moving up to a special link covering all types of spare work. On reaching this link he would have a firing instructor to ride with him on a passenger train to observe his capabilities. The special link was the most anti-social link at the depot where driver and fireman alike had to hold themselves available for duty for ten hours from a given time, without any financial compensation. Imagine what it was like hanging around home for ten hours, afraid to go out for a hair cut or do an errand in case you missed the call boy, and lost a day's pay. This was the way the private company treated its staff in the interests of economy.

Step 5

After passing through the special link, the next move was to a freight link, i.e. Wychnor–Burton–Rugeley–Wolverhampton–Dudley and Stour Valley.

Step 6

All links above the freight link were passenger links through which the drivers and firemen progressed as vacancies arose. The one exception in these links was the double-trip link where the drivers were volunteers. They stayed in the link until retirement, but the firemen progressed through the passenger duties. The drawback to this link was the unsociable hours, as they had only one full week day turn, 5.25 a.m. on Lichfield Trip 252. The rest of the turns were as follows:

8.15 p.m. Camdens – double trip
7.43 a.m. Wellington's double trip (two turns)
2.30 p.m. Water Orton – Crewe (fruit) two turns – double trip
12.20 p.m. Staffords via Cannock line – double trip

Step 7

As firemen progressed through the links they would eventually be passed out for driving duties by a loco inspector, who would test their knowledge on rules and regulations. They would have a practical test and ride with them on a passenger and freight train. They would now be classed as a passed fireman.

Step 8

Registered driver - after being registered as a driver he would go through the same sequence as he did as a fireman.

Career at Ryecroft Shed (Closed to Steam, Easter 1957) and Subsequent Posts

Started work at Ryecroft (Junior caller up)	21 April 1930
Suspended due to recession (Walsall)	20 July 1932
Re-engaged (caller up, Walsall)	17 February 1934
Made a cleaner (Walsall)	19 November 1934
Made a fireman (Walsall)	30 August 1937
Made a driver (transfer – Bushbury)	11 February 1952
Driver (transfer – back to Walsall)	22 November 1954
Ryecroft closed to steam (DMU Units)	Easter 1957
Transferred surplus staff to Bescot	9 June 1958
Returned as DMU Driver (Walsall)	10 August 1959
Ryecroft Depot closed entirely	15 February 1965
Driver (transferred to Bescot)	15 February 1965
WHS Diesel Instructor Driver until (Bescot)	2 December 1974
Traction Inspector at Leamington	2 December 1974

Traction Inspector at Saltley until retirement	10 October 1975
Retired at sixty-five	27 August 1980

RATES OF PAY.	£	*s*	*d*
Caller up rate of pay when started	0	13	4 per week
Cleaner rate	2	8	0
After 313 firing turns	2	17	0
After 626 firing turns	3	6	0
After another 313 firing turns	3	12	0
Rate of pay when married was	3	12	0
Top rate driving pay	4	10	0

Jack Reynolds Jnr, Ryecroft Shed 1904 to 1956

In 1879, Jack Reynolds's father had walked from Cannock to Ryecroft shed to seek employment at the new L&NWR shed which replaced its South Staffs Railway predecessor. Jack Snr was successful and became a reliable servant to the company, finally becoming a driver. Young Jack, born in 1888, was eager to follow in his father's footsteps and, being accepted on his father's recommendation, started his own career at the shed in 1904 at the age of sixteen. He lived with his family in rented accommodation at 45, William Street, in the Butts district near to the shed, and remained there until finally passing away in 1980 at the age of ninety-two. Jack started his career doing the basic and mundane tasks of a young cleaner: sweeping up, tea making and calling-up duties. Soon becoming a regular cleaner with a pay of 16*s* a week, he could add to this on occasions by coaling engines by hand, the rate for coaling engines then being 6*d* per ton. His normal working hours were sixty per week. The shed's allocation at this time was Webb's standardised L&NWR classes, typically 'Cauliflower' 0-6-0s, coal engines, 2-4-2 and 0-6-2 tank engines and saddle tank shunters with open footplates.

For relaxation, and production of wholesome home-grown food, his father rented an allotment situated between the old South Staffordshire line and the Midland line. There were then several such plots near Mill Lane bridge, adjacent to the shed. Jack Snr's territory was protected by a wooden fence, with several very sturdy high posts inserted along its length as strengtheners, these always being surmounted by glass bottles. Sited to catch the attention of the firemen who passed by the allotment every few minutes, the crews rose to the sporting challenge and tried to smash the bottles with the only ammunition immediately available – sizeable lumps of coal. Subsequently, on each visit to his patch, among healthy and thriving rows of potatoes, cabbages and peas, were many examples of carbon fruit, to ensure a roaring fire and a warm living room during the long, cold of winter – very welcome. Yet another legal Ryecroft initiative that broke no law.

One pleasant sight Jack remembers as a young man was viewing, from either allotment or the shed confines, the impressive passing each morning of a Johnson 4-2-2 spinner single-wheel locomotive, descending at speed from Lichfield Road Junction to Walsall Station, the loco and its gas-lit clerestory coaches in immaculate crimson red livery, the train coming from Redditch to Walsall via Birmingham New Street.

It was 1908 before Jack had his first opportunity to fire a locomotive off shed. As a result of staff sickness, he enjoyed two weeks on the flat shunt at Norton Junction, breaking up and reassembling coal trains coming in from Cannock Chase. Jack and his driver were among the last Ryecroft men to work a train from Norton Junction to Walsall Wood Colliery during this fortnight. From 1 January the colliery acquired their own shunting locos, which then brought the coal to a siding situated to the rear of Norton junction No.1 signal box. Promotion in those days was slow, with drivers often continuing well after their sixty-fifth birthday, now considered the age of retirement. From 1910 he was fortunate to be rostered a few firing turns, always at first on local shunting duties.

In 1911, when on locomotive disposal and turning duties on shed, he often had the difficult and unwelcome task of coaling and watering the steam Sentinel railcar that was Ryecroft-based for a period of trial running on the Cannock Branch, from Walsall to Rugeley. Not much thought had been put into the mechanics of daily servicing of the unit, which resembled a passenger carriage, but had a small steam locomotive built in. The restricted access to the small interior bunker demanded that each lump of coal had to be stored away by hand from a nearby coal wagon – a lengthy, boring and filthy procedure. To make matters worse, the feed bag from most water columns was incompatible with the small filler cap fitted, and a small bore hose took ages to fill the unit's tank. After about twelve months the railcar was transferred away, much to the relief of Ryecroft men, who had found its abilities taxed on the 1 in 70 and 1 in 80 gradients of the route to Rugeley.

In 1912 Jack became victim of a longstanding L&NWR staff flexibility system, by which Midlands men were allocated to both North Wales and Fylde coast sheds to reinforce their footplate staff for the hectic activity of the summer season. The system was reversed in winter when 'supernumerary' (as they were called) staff at these depots were allocated to the Midlands for increased traffic in the coal-producing areas. Jack was asked to volunteer for summertime duties at Bangor, and with no alternative except dismissal, he accepted the invitation to the seaside. He found it to be no holiday and often worked fifteen hours a day. As was usual, he had to find his own lodgings, his base being the top floor attic of a local railwayman's house at 12*s* 6*d* a week for bed and breakfast. Other meals had to be paid for and he had to do his own washing. Working whatever hours were possible, his wage was just over £1 a week, enabling him to keep 3*s* (15p) pocket money and to send 5*s* home to his mother.

Jack's previous experience consisted of firing shunting engines, his new job being in a link firing local and express services between Holyhead, Chester, Manchester and Liverpool – a bit of a shock and one that took some getting used to. After a long daily battle with several tons of coal, L&NWR locos had a reputation for being heavy on the commodity; all Jack wanted to do on return to Bangor was to go to bed and sleep. Undaunted, he was soon at ease with the new routine, and if he was lucky he might get one day off to go round the town and enjoy the bracing sea air. Every six weeks he could manage two days at home with the aid of a free pass or quarter-fare concessions.

One duty he remembered vividly was to relieve the crew of a Holyhead–Manchester express arriving at Bangor at 8.00 a.m., stopping at Chester and Warrington. The locomotive was an 'Alfred the Great' or a 'Renown'. On arrival at Manchester, he and his driver took charge of a similar loco to work a non-stop express to Liverpool, arriving

LNWR loco 2055 on Ryecroft shed prior to working a Walsall to Camden freight in 1908. The small lad is Jack Reynolds. (Jack Reynolds, Jack Haddock Collection)

after midday. After a break for a meal they then worked a Liverpool–Bangor semi-fast, stopping at all major stations, being relieved by Holyhead men at Bangor around 9 p.m. He also worked local trains to many inland North Wales stations now long disappeared from the railway map in this age of the motor car. One day Jack was summoned to the Bangor foreman's office to inform him he would be firing on the Amlwch motor train as the regular fireman was sick. This pleasant and easy task was a push-pull job, leisurely pacing across the Isle of Anglesey, the motive power being a Webb 2-4-2 'Chopper' tank. The duty entailed a unique experience which he would never have met again in his railway career. As no water column was available at Amlwch, the driver had to give him instructions on how to operate a steam pump attached to the locomotive frame, as water at the Isle's terminal station had to be retrieved from a deep well by a small bore hose – a time consuming and slow process.

Jack returned to the North Wales coast for the 1913 summer service in what turned out to be a far less physical routine. This time he was allocated to Llandudno Junction on local services, mainly on 18in Webb 'Cauliflower' 0-6-0s. A feature of the line side often seen in summer was the charred embankments. The tall-chimney Webb locomotives, when really opened out, could produce some spectacular firework displays with red-hot char emitted skywards, to fall as small pyrotechnic bombs. These were often blamed by the local landowners for the accidental 'scorched earth' policy. Most farmers grain crops were sown in fields away from the tracks, more adventurous farmers learning the hard way, lodging claims for compensation against the L&NWR. Jack enjoyed the two years he spent on 'foreign' soil despite the hard work and isolation, but always insisted in later years that all the railway companies knew how to get blood out of a stone.

His Welsh experience reflected on him favourably as he was promoted to a regular fireman for the winter of 1913. Although the railway management were considered martinets, they did favour flexible servants. Proving his worth, Jack was later to hold the regulator at Ryecroft until 1956. Jack fired shunting and freight locos until the outbreak of the Frist World War, working on passenger services as other Ryecroft personnel joined the colours. One such demanding job was a balanced passenger working between Walsall and Stoke over the North Staffordshire Railway. His previous work over the Cannock branch sometimes allowed him fleeting visions of a brown 'Knotty' (nickname for the North Staffordshire Railway) tank locomotive. Such an apparition failed at Walsall station one day, having to retire to Ryecroft for repair. Its good looks and large Staffordshire Knot embellishment on the side tanks, together with its immaculate turn out, turned one or two heads. Ryecroft, as ever, had the last word with some typical down-to-earth quips such as 'handsome is as handsome does', a comment on its failure.

When Jack fired his first turn on the return Stoke working, he again experienced the L&NWR's expectation of its men. Jack and his driver booked on at 12.30 p.m. to be allocated a Webb 2-4-2 Chopper tank, already prepared. Leaving the shed they drifted down to Platform 1 in Walsall Station to pick up the six-wheeled non-corridor stock, which left at 1 p.m. Onwards from Colwich (just north of Rugeley), Ryecroft men had been trained to work the 'Knotty' to Stoke. Likewise, Stoke men knew the road to Walsall. On arrival at Stoke, Jack had to uncouple his loco to couple up to a Stafford local from Stoke, the North Staffs crew taking over the working from Walsall. Again a run of a very few miles saw a Stafford arrival before detaching to retire to Stafford shed for water, servicing and snap. At 4.15 p.m. they left with a local to Stoke, arriving in time to work the 6 p.m. Stoke to New Street. From here they finally worked a local back to Walsall before arrival at Ryecroft at about 11 p.m., having stopped at almost fifty stations during the shift.

During the war Jack fired in several Ryecroft links, managing to start driving in early 1918 as a passed fireman. This meant being in charge of shunting and freight locos. To qualify for a driver's position he had to acquire the experience of working 115 brake van turns on mineral or coal trains on the mainline with guards vans attached, acquiring this experience often as replacement for sick or unavailable drivers. The magic number was achieved on 23 June 1920, but pay-wise it was not until February 1921 that he became an official Ryecroft driver with a wage of 14*s* a day, only to be kidded at the depot that he would soon become a 'Top hat' driver. Since Victorian times there was a tradition among engine drivers, when having attained seniority and experience at about the age of sixty and before retirement, to proclaim their status. This was to dress well and wear the top hat when out on the town. The symbol lifted their ego in order to mix with gentry and businessmen at theatres and hotel bars in local towns. The few Ryecroft men who adopted the practice enjoyed the notoriety, but endured comments from the rank and file, with some caustic deflating delivery meant to be overheard. All meant to keep them within easy reach of those yet to make their mark on the footplate. The first turn Jack Reynolds worked as a driver was on 24 June 1920 on the Walsall Long Street shunt, his mount being the open-cab Webb saddle tank engine 3153, on the 4.00 a.m. till 2 p.m. shift.

Several Ryecroft drivers worked trains to the coastal resorts, but Jack Reynolds was perhaps the only one who worked trains over the sea, to Anglesey.

Jack Stanley

Jack Stanley joined the Midland Railway at the start of his lifetime's commitment to a career on the railway. His dedication to the Midland, of course, saw him belong to the Midland Brotherhood, embracing its ways and philosophies, its methods and attitudes. This naturally included its bitter rivalry with the London North Western Railway, with which it was in intense competition. The two great companies met at Walsall, the L&NWR imposing itself as the first among equals in Walsall after the grouping of 1923. By 1925 the Midland Railway shed at Walsall was closed and all resources were centred in the L&NWR Ryecroft shed, Jack joining the opposition without malice or regret, which was only to be expected of a totally dedicated and professional railwayman. He would have taken a great deal of banter, but could, and did, hold his own with dignity to be accepted as one of Ryecroft's own.

Jack served with the South Staffordshire Regiment in France during the First World War. His bravery and humanity was rewarded as he selflessly recovered a seriously wounded officer from the battlefield during heavy and prolonged artillery and rifle fire. This operation in Pigeon Wood, near Arras in France, was to earn him the Military Medal for gallantry under fire. His long and distinguished railway career came to an end as he retired from railway service at Ryecroft in 1958. Professional in everything he did for the Midland, LMS and British Railways, he was highly regarded and respected by management and his colleagues.

Jack Steele

Trade, business and employment hit a trough after the First World War. Many men returned from the traumatisation of the trenches, the rigours and disciplines of army life, to find that the promised ideal of a brave new world (plenty, prosperity and permanent employment), never materialised. Matters got worse and culminated in the hard times of years of Depression. With many businesses failing, and men often on short-time working, the railways which had transported the machinery of war and its raw materials in prodigious tonnage, found themselves with overcapacity and overstaffing. The railway itself was suffering a siege mentality like the returning troops of the Somme and Marne.

Jack Steele was one of the fortunate ones. His application for railway service was accepted after the usual interview, and he began work as a cleaner and call-up boy at Bescot in the late 1920s, living with his parents in Mill Street, adjacent to Ryecroft shed. The Walsall area, a stronghold of leather manufacturers and saddlery, had been buoyant producing thousands of horse and mule harnesses for wartime, but post-war reflected the prevailing Depression of the Black Country, the Midlands and the national trend. Unemployment or reduced hours of work affected money in the pocket, little being available for travel, seaside holidays or day trips. Railway activity was therefore 'flat' in economic terms, both passenger and freight.

Like any employment agency, the railways monitered their employees with regard to attitude, ability, time-keeping, reliability and promotional prospects. Jack applied for Ryecroft to become his home shed. Being young, flexible, capable and of good report, he became a passed cleaner in the early 1930s firing shunting locomotives in the busy Bescot yard. It was to be some years in the future before he became a resident at Ryecroft shed. Indeed, he seemed destined to be moved about 'from pillow to post' as enforced transfers were proposed to other areas of the country when vacancies occurred. To have refused such moves would have automatically meant dismissal – the sack!

Jack was ordered to report immediately to Bath on the Somerset & Dorset Railway to fill a vacancy there until further notice. On arrival his first task was to find living accomodation. The company never made arrangements on the men's behalf, but this was usually solved at the new shed, where local railwaymen would put up a fellow railwayman for a reasonable rate of board and lodging. On average digs would account for about 29*s* 6*d* (£1.47p) of the standard fireman's wage of 37*s* 6*d* (£1.87p), which left little to be spent, saved or sent home.

After about twelve months firing in the Mendips, the economic situation in the country got worse, and I suppose a 'last in, first out' policy was practised and Jack was ordered to report to Wembley, London. Here there was a job available as a porter. Nearer the capital the cost of living was found to be dearer, and the porter's wage less than that of a locomotive fireman. His stay at Wembley lasted nine months, where he would daily have viewed the company's principal express power hurtling past on prestigious high-speed trains. These would have included the Royal and Midday Scots, the Birmingham two-hour expresses and the heavy Liverpool turns. He must have been left to wonder if his footplate career could be continued, and when.

Good news came when he was 'requested' to transfer to Bristol Bath Road. For this transfer he had to travel to Bristol via Birmingham, although the route to Bristol from Paddington was quicker. The LMS was certainly not going to pay money to the rival GWR (Great Western Railway) when its own trains could be used. A journey 'on the cushions' allowed him to take in the line-side features of the West Coast Mainline, including the massive Tring Cutting and that subterranean mine called Kilsby Tunnel, before reaching Rugby on his way to 'Brum'. The wait for a connection at busy New Street was a joy as he contemplated the longlost feel of a firing shovel, an insatiable firebox and a mountain of coal to be moved daily. He was to be back on the footplate at last! Jack worked from Bristol for approximately two years, which passed quickly as Bath Road's citizenry gradually deciphered the new language and accepted 'the Brummie' as one of their own. Often working trains to Birmingham and Sheffield, he booked off at Saltley shed and could travel the few miles home before his rostered return duty to the West. Just as he felt settled at Bristol, he was ordered to report back to Bath shed for continued battle with Masbury Summit and other daunting inclines on the steeply undulating Somerset & Dorset route. Although firing turns to Bournemouth were sometimes available, his second spell at Bath Green Park involved more restricted local, shunting and freight work as he was out-based at Radstock or Highbridge for short spells.

After almost five years of wandering during these difficult years, which involved several and varied lodging arrangements, the exile was recalled to a regular firing post at Ryecroft, a settled life and eventually council-house accommodation. At last a place he could call home. By 1936 there seemed to be the prospect, indeed inevitability, of further conflict with Germany, and Jack Steele and the Ryecroft fraternity were never again uncertain of full-time employment. There was a saying at 3C that security and an increased pay packet were possible thanks to Adolf Hitler. During the second European confrontation, Jack and his mates found traffic demands never imagined in their wildest dreams. The old order at Ryecroft, the Midland-derived 4Fs and the 'Super D' 0-8-0s battled manfully on and proved their worth and, although Stanier's superb 4-6-0s were available, none were allocated to 3C until after the war. Webb 1P 2-4-2Ts, Fowler 3P 2-6-2Ts and Stanier 2-6-4Ts handled the passenger duties.

Jack and the other Ryecroft staff survived the storm of war and generally accepted the nationalisation of the railways in 1948. He graduated to the left-hand side of the cab as a driver of Ryecroft's steam fleet until the depot's closure for steam traction in 1957. The shed was converted to a diesel multiple-unit shed until its final demise in 1965. One last fling of fate saw him transferred a couple of miles away to Bescot (3A) depot until his 1973 retirement.

Perhaps Jack's railway career could be considered exceptional, convoluted and highly uncertain. To many, this trauma could have caused family difficulty and complex social consequences. Jack, however, was philosophical, accepting the fact that he had been shunted into several sidings, bay platforms and foreign parts in his career. He wisely accepted his moves as necessary in difficult times, and looked on it all as valuable experience, which in his younger years was tolerable, educative and would stand him in good stead. He believed the management recognised his dedication and flexibility to the company service he signed up to as a youth. He eventually got a permanent placement at home, and, as a senior Ryecroft man, could always refer to his exile years should any of the young ones moan about unsociable hours, difficult shifts, long hours and graft, telling them to shut up and get the job done! After all his experiences, they were lucky to have a good, secure job based in their home town, and a stable career which was missing in his early life and much appreciated when it finally became available.

Jim Barnett

Just after the Second World War, Jim Barnett, then a Ryecroft fireman, was rostered for duty early on the morning of the August Bank Holiday. As he was not allocated to a specific job he was acting in the spare link, which could mean he could fire any locomotive on either local or long-distance work should a need arise. Often it could mean a day pottering around the shed, but in any emergency, which included illness, breakdown, de-railed locos or stock, or any extra traffic not catered for, the 'spare' men were immediately allocated the duty. At such a busy time, passenger stock not needed for service could be sent anywhere to cover special duties, excursions, troop trains or any other contingency at short notice. On this Bank Holiday, Jim was allocated a duty to fire an empty stock train from New Mills carriage sidings to Crewe, so helping to get the coaches some way towards their destination to cover an unforeseen need further north. Jim and his driver were allocated an ex-L&NWR G2A freight 0-8-0, No.8905, as the depot's regular passenger engines were obviously engaged in excursion work and seasonal

View of Ryecroft Junction from Butts bridge showing the BR-designed signal box, 1958. (Jack Haddock Collection)

traffic to the seaside resorts and local beauty spots. Such was the congestion that it was some hours after their departure from Walsall that they eventually ran into Crewe South yard at Basford Hall. Thinking this was the end of their duty, they were about to uncouple to run to the shed at Crewe South to be turned for home, when they were informed by the yard inspector that the empty stock was destined for Carlisle. They were also informed of a shortage of motive power and crews, and that control had requested that the old 'Super D' should continue its journey to Preston. A Crewe South driver was available for this trip (Jim's driver was not 'passed' for the road north of Crewe) and Jim was requested to fire to Preston, which he did, having the incentive of 'overtime'.

The old girl was not stretched by the load and would amble along steadily at about 30 to 40mph, with the class's usual side to side front-end motion. The firing needed was not heavy, but many delays were experienced after leaving the four-track section north of Crewe. They had to wait for excursion and mainline traffic priorities at the well-known bottlenecks of Warrington and Wigan, where traffic from the Welsh coast and from Manchester was dense. Blackpool, Morecambe and Furness line traffic from Lancashire and Yorkshire could at times be quite chaotic, especially on a Bank Holiday. Having to wait for suitable gaps in the traffic, Preston was eventually reached. On arrival at the important junction for the Fylde coast, they were told that no relief was available and that they were to carry on to Carlisle, after filling the tender with water from yet another trackside column with its heavy leather bag.

Never in his wildest dreams had Jim thought that his duty would include firing over Grayrigg and the redoubtable obstacle of Shap incline on a Ryecroft 'Super D', or any other loco for that matter. No.8905 would have to be pushed as fast as the old freighter could realistically be expected to go in order to prevent obstruction of high-speed traffic on the twin tracks. They expected a routine of continuous quick dashes followed by strategic retreat to reserved tracks, where they could be overtaken by the 'Jubilees', 'Scots', 'Patriots' and 'Duchesses' hard at work on the 'varnish' (a railway nickname for express passenger trains on account of the highly varnished stock), allowing the veteran to recover its breath before its next foray along the 'Main'. Taking in the dramatic scenery of the Lune Gorge between short, sharp bursts of heavy firing, Jim was enjoying the vagaries of 3C's spare link, finally to top Shap, to begin the long-promised lighter firing on the long descent to the border town. The crew rolled into Carlisle having almost emptied the tender, Jim having, by that time, been firing for almost twelve hours.

The 'D's' crewmen were relieved at Carlisle to return 'on the cushions' on the next southbound express, which arrived at Citadel (the name of Carlisle's station) almost immediately, and so were not able to witness what happened to old No.8905 and its stock. Its return to Ryecroft did not happen until some weeks later and it was rumoured that the old 0-8-0 was refuelled and eventually worked as far as Glasgow. If this was the case, it certainly would have been a record for a Ryecroft freight engine. In any case, the 'Super D' was welcomed home as a willing long-distance wayfarer, becoming almost a celebrity. From the seats on his return journey home, Jim was able to enjoy the wild, windswept isolation of Shap Fell, the high-speed flight down Grayrigg and the pleasant countryside between Lancaster and Preston. He wished there was to be more long-distance work to come in his Ryecroft career, perhaps the 'Camdens', but the 'Birchills shunt' was more logical than his fantasy dreams. However, his next pay packet was more interesting.

Jim Riley, 1900–1974, Steam Locomotive Driver, Ryecroft and Bescot 1915 to 1965

Jim Riley was a Rushall man, Rushall being a village just outside Walsall, but still close to Ryecroft shed. He joined the L&NWR in 1915 and progressed through the ranks of cleaner, fireman and driver to eventually become a top-link driver. All railway promotion was, of course, dependent on time served, experience and, far more importantly, opportunity. Jim enjoyed his job and was hard working and methodical. The latter trait saw him keeping records of each day of his working life – times, experiences and his destinations – a wealth of detail of his job and its demands, a veritable treasure trove of information, today much valued because of its rarity.

Some of the facts and figures about wages and working practices from former times seem incredible today. Jim's main boast about his fifty years' working life on the railway was that he was never out of work, even through the worst of the Depression years. He felt the job he did was important and respected the responsibility he was entrusted with. He never went to work without a collar and tie, which was not the norm for the average working man at that time, and certainly not often seen on the footplate in steam days.

When the 1920 slump came, 106 men were made redundant at Ryecroft. Because Jim was at this time in the 'special link', generally experienced men having authority to journey over a wide operating range of routes and duties, he was retained. But, as he remembered in later life, it was a close thing. He recollects that if another three men had to be made redundant, he would have been included. The fact that he was a young, strong fireman paired with an 'old hand', being diligent, resourceful and a fine prospect for the future, had been his salvation. In 1933–34, many more men had to leave 3C, being sent to other sheds and non-motive power positions all over the country. Many returned to Ryecroft later as improving economic conditions and trade allowed, motive power demands being increased steadily to former levels of activity.

Jim was married in 1932 to a Wednesbury girl, Selina, who was 'in service' to a family in Handsworth Wood, and then to the Smith family in Buchanan Road, Walsall. His wage at this time was £2 10*s* 0*d* per week, from which he paid his 2*s* 9*d*. Selina soon found that the life of a railwayman was not as regulated and routine as the households she had served in. Shifts known as 'double trips' were a regular occurrence for special link, which meant Jim would often be away for more than one day at a time. Staying at railway lodges overnight meant taking your own food with you, and Selina quickly became used to packing bacon, eggs, lard, tea and sugar and so on in a wicker basket designed to hold the food and necessary tackle, and which was of such design that it would fit behind the saddle of his bicycle for the journey to the sheds.

When Jim was a fireman he had to do 313 firing turns to become a top rate fireman, and then two years at an extra shilling a day, plus two more years at a further shilling a day. On some days he would be subjected to 'trip rates', which meant that however long it took to complete the duty he still got the standard rate paid for the job. Often a ten-hour trip rate job could take well over ten hours to complete, due to route congestion, failures or diversions and operational difficulties. On a good job, however, it could take less than ten hours with payment guaranteed for the ten-hour duty. In these early days a top-rate driver earned a basic £3 12*s* 0*d* a week.

In his days at Ryecroft (1915–1943) Jim would often have his 'snap basket' taken to him while he was at work. It was considered a family treat to take his basket to the railway where it passed the bottom of Cartbridge Lane in Rushall, known locally as the 'sixty steps' bridge, and pass the food to him as the locomotive was halted momentarily by the bridge.

A railwayman's duties were extremely varied and took them over a wide area, and many were the stories of both funny and tragic occurrences experienced in their daily work. Jim was no exception and his family recalled some of them at a family gathering shortly after he retired. One such story was told, of a dog which was being transported in the guard's van of a local passenger train. During the stop at Dudley Port Station the dog escaped and ran off along the platform, closely followed by the guard who was screaming, 'Stop that dog, it's a parcel!', much to the merriment of the onlookers. To explain, railway companies were happy to transport dogs or other animals, and for charging purposes they were classed as parcels. It was also a condition that there was someone to collect them at their destination.

Sadly, other stories involved the frequent suicide attempts experienced as desperate people jumped in front of trains. Some would jump off bridges in front of the locomotive, with train crews helpless with the situation beyond their control, but confronted by the gory situation when the train braked to a standstill. An eerie story involved Jim stopping a train during the night in wartime, as it approached Birmingham. He said he never knew why he did it, it just felt that it was someone else who applied the brakes. He jumped down from the engine to the track to look around, and 15 yards in front of the engine a bridge had been bombed, and the track was no longer there. His comment at the time was typically phlegmatic, 'it was enough to turn you religious'.

Jim's experiences were written down daily in a book for the last twenty-five years of his working life – times worked and destinations recorded, overtime worked and, similarly, 'rest' days worked. The record was updated at the end of the working day and gave a very graphic picture of the erratic pattern of shifts a railwayman was expected to endure. The first question his children asked whenever they got home from school or play was, 'Is Dad in bed?'. If the answer was positive they had to be quiet. The record in the book revealed evidence of many eighty hours plus working weeks, which would not be tolerated today, and could even be considered a highly dangerous risk.

Anything not work related had to be extremely special to be entered in his book, such as when his daughter and son got married, his father's funeral and the date when he had a new dog. Also recorded were the dates of all his statutory medicals, which had to be undertaken by all footplate employees at regular intervals. Eyesight tests were critical. The cover of the book contained recipes for cough mixture, a secret concoction for making hydrangeas a better blue colour, and, more normally, medical and National Insurance numbers. The highly individualistic book provided a unique record of a quarter of a century's involvement in railway service based at Walsall. Jim's highly interesting compilation was eventually donated to the Local History department in Walsall. Tragically, no trace of this book can now be found in Walsall's Archive. (Information from Mavis Riley.)

Northern Lights Bill Bate

Billy Bate's L&NWR career as a Ryecroft employee was notably unique. His pre-war experience driving the L&NWR experimental buses linking Brownhills and Hednesford stations (recorded elsewhere in this volume), and his overseas wartime service as an ambulance driver, were followed by a return to Ryecroft at the end of hostilities until his retirement in 1954. Bill was not only a very competent engineman, he had a bent for things mechanical. He had an inventive and analytical mind and a resolve to get the best out of the machines he operated. These personal attributes perhaps explain why he was selected to drive the pioneer buses together with Sid Broughton and Sid Hayes. The 1913 experimental service used buses which, although solidly built with heavy duty chassis and chain drive, were not entirely reliable in operation. Their petrol engine and its associated electrical systems could be subject to the vagaries of the weather. Chain drive, although rugged and simple in operation, had its own problems of tensioning, maintenance and lubrication. 'Wear and tear' and the primitive road surfaces of the time with their deep potholes, could result in breakages and delays. A 'driver mechanic' was more able to get the best out of the resources available, thus cutting down on operational costs and 'down-time inefficiency'.

During his railway driving career, he came across locomotives in all states of mechanical condition – locos that were running sweetly after major overhaul at Crewe works, to those already having had several light and intermediate repairs and now in the state of 'awaiting shops', with rough riding, big-ends knocking and poor steaming. These locos were taken off mainline duties to eke out a few more miles as heavy-duty shunters and yard engines before a further recall to 'shops' for boiler renewal and replacement repairs which could almost be considered a total rebuild.

Bill liked experimentation, especially with locos known to be poor and erratic steamers, and often used scrap metal to make improvised tools to improve steam efficiency. These included blast pipe 'jimmies' which were inserted into the blast pipe assemblies in the locomotive's smoke-box, in effect a metal washer which restricted the blast pipe orifice, so creating a sharper exhaust and, consequently, an increased volume of air sucked into the firebox to aid combustion and a more fuel-efficient economy. Officially frowned upon by top management, such practice was often undertaken both by shed staff and a few drivers. His enquiring mind led to the improvement of the standard issue 'Aladdin' oil lamp and to lubricating oil-can extensions to facilitate oiling, especially in the notoriously cramped spaces which had to be accessed between locomotive frames to lubricate the valve gear and motion of inside-cylinder locomotives. The Fowler 2-6-2T engines, for many years operating from Ryecroft, were notoriously poor performers, being steam shy and poorly thought of – a reputation which spread countrywide and a problem which was never cured, but no doubt the problem was given Bill's careful attention. While Bill was struggling with the lifeless somnolence of Fowler 3P No.17's wayward shortcomings one night in January 1938, most of northern England witnessed the most spectacular display of the phenomenon known as the Aurora Borealis or Northern Lights. On this particular night of much enhanced electro-magnetic activity, Billy Bate was approaching the end of his shift. Reporting for duty at Ryecroft at 2.30 p.m., No.17 was eased down to Walsall station light engine, where it was coupled up to three non-corridor coaches which were situated in the middle road. These were to be shunted into Platform 2 in readiness to work a local passenger train to Birmingham via Soho. On arrival at New Street, the diagram continued with a journey to Rugeley Trent Valley (all stations), arriving around 5.30 p.m. with a consequent return to Walsall, after light shunting duties.

After the passengers had alighted, Billy Bate shunted No.17 back onto the middle road while he and his mate had a meal break before another local was worked to New Street. During his break between 9.00 and 9.30 p.m., the driver was aware of the brilliant dancing lights of the Aurora in the night sky and, being a keen photographer, decided to take 'French leave' from duty to dash to pick up his trusted Ross Ensign camera from his Webster Road home, about a mile from the station. Borrowing one of the many railwaymen's cycles from a cycle rack on the up side of Platform 1 and noting the absence of the station inspector, Bill informed his fireman to cover his desertion of a locomotive on duty and belted home at a great rate of knots to return with his camera, replace the borrowed machine and rejoin the footplate, relieved to find that his absence had gone unnoticed. Having already worked out a plan of action, No.17 and its train were returned to the platform face for a late trip to Birmingham, followed by an all-stations job to Lichfield Trent Valley. Away from the bright lights of the city centre on leaving Four Oaks, Bill was approaching open country and realised that the heavenly display was getting even more spectacular.

At Trent Valley the duty ceased, approaching midnight. The crew had to run round the train and the photograph would be taken before the empty stock was forwarded to

Ryecroft loco No.17 during the Aurora Borealis at Brownhills, 1938, as related in the text by Billy Bates. (Bill Bates)

Walsall Pleck carriage sidings. However, they were immediately given a clear road, and in consternation Bill thought he had lost his chance of recording the historic occasion. Passing through Brownhills station they went under Chester Road bridge to be halted by a red light alongside Brownhills goods yard. Bill sent his fireman to the signal-box to carry out the rule 55 regulations, the fireman coming back to the footplate with the news of a very long wait due to extended shunting movements across the mainline at Norton Junction, the cause being a complicated manoeuvre by a long coal train from the Norton Branch.

Although it would mean a late finish, this was the break he had hoped for to get the possibility of a picture of a lifetime. No.17 and its coaches were used to good effect as the picture was composed, the display normally best seen within the Arctic Circle, being taken before the green signal was given for a road back to Walsall. Bill developed and printed the photograph taken on Agfa film and using Agfa paper, the result not only being good, but of archival interest. As a small boy of twelve living at 78, Webster Road, opposite Bill Bate at No.77, I was shown the photograph and over the years forgot about it. Bill continued his duties at Ryecroft and retired in 1954 at the age of sixty-five. In 1956 Bill passed away and, beginning my involvement with photography, I was given Bill's enlarger and what was left of his negatives and photographs. No.17 and the coaching set were enlarged to a 15in x 12in print, and it remains in Walsall Borough Archives as possibly the only photograph of the 1938 'Aurora Borealis'.

If the opportunity re-occurred today, much of the impact of the dancing skies would be lost due to the glare of intense modern street lighting. Bill, fortunately, had only a few feeble gas lamps to contend with for his picture of a lifetime.

Driver Colin Mould, 'Off again, On again!'

Requests to transfer in times of recession on the railways were not always long-distance appointments. One such transfer was a 'foreign' driver who came to 3C as a young man from nearby Uttoxeter. Originating from the rural backwater amidst rolling cattle country, the new recruit was, by the time of this anecdote, middle-aged and a driver. He was quiet and unassuming in nature, and his speech still reflected a country upbringing with

Ryecroft-based diesel multiple unit working a Lichfield to Birmingham service, Shenstone station, 1959. (Jack Haddock Collection)

liberal use of 'thee', 'thou' and 'thy'. This was in marked contrast to the sharper Walsall, happy-go-lucky repartee of witty banter with a fun-loving outlook. Colin Mould had suffered under driver Sim Foster as fireman, and his driving technique had been strongly influenced by the old master. Colin became a wide-open regulator man like his tutor, and didn't hang about. His exuberance caused a few problems at Ryecroft, with derailments and incidents somewhat above average for 3C drivers. His report sheets handed in after mishaps were thorough, detailed and lengthy, and eventually the accrued paperwork resulted in an enforced visit to the office.

There were to be no more 'offs'. All paperwork was to be kept to a minimum – accurate, simple and concise, and limited to one sheet of paper. For a time the huge man's record was exemplary, until, most unfortunately and beyond his control, while working a goods train a weak and well-worn point blade gave way under his engine while shunting. The incident again demanded putting pen to paper. With his previous caution still embedded in his mind, his carefully considered response was a cryptic one-liner, 'Off again, on again, gone again'. Deposited in the office in an open tray, the missive soon became the focus of unauthorised eyes. Within a very short time laughter could be heard from small groups of men around the shed as work stopped and shed staff rolled about in uncontrolled merriment. The audacity of their new hero was unexpected. Colin had excelled himself – a new legend was born. If he hadn't already got a nickname, he had now, and his new monika 'off again, on again', stuck with him for the rest of his Ryecroft life.

It was known that the point was an accident waiting to happen and had been reported several times before. He was therefore totally exonerated from blame, and only minor murmurings were forthcoming from the office, who had to acknowledge that their requests on the format of his report had been followed to their guidelines. No charges of over-zealous reaction were forthcoming. Quiet and unassuming he might still be, but a few years at Walsall had sharpened his outlook and humour considerably. He was now willing and able to give as good as he got. He was finally accepted into the brotherhood of 'characters', which was a feature of Ryecroft life, its community a 'broad church', the unexpected being an almost daily occurrence. Colin's one-liner was talked about occasionally until the shed's closure.

Picking Up The Train by Ken Horan

Ken Horan was once instructed by the Ryecroft shed inside foreman to go with a driver to relieve an 'out of hours' crew coming into Walsall station. There was plenty of time in hand for the half-mile walk, and although Tommy Deakin's pub (the driver's local) would be bypassed en route, the driver, who liked his beer, decided to call at Ma Male's 'Dun Cow' at the top of Park Street. This was situated by the Savoy Cinema, which was only a matter of yards from the station concourse. The beer was got in and consumed, but during the drink the driver's eye had been taken by a female seated nearby. The driver took a fancy to her and went over for a chat, to return to Ken to state that he would be away for a few minutes, and to 'get yourself another drink'.

A little later the driver returned, striding purposefully to Ken's table and obviously in a hurry, although over ten minutes was still available to get to the platforms. 'Drink yer beer up', he said somewhat briskly, 'Let's get going. She thinks I've given her a ten bob note, but it was a Wrong Line Order'. The drink was finished in two or three gulps, the Ryecroft men gliding through the pub door to join the anonymity of the groups of passing shoppers to pick up their allotted train as though nothing had happened.

Frank Rigby, Ryecroft Shed 'Awayday' for Fitting Staff, 1930 to 1945

Frank Rigby passed away in 1979 after dedicating his working life to the London Midland & Scottish Railway, and later British Railways and British Rail. Starting work as a fitter's apprentice in 1930, he progressed through the grades to become senior fitter at Ryecroft shed (3C), remaining at the depot until 1946. He then served in a similar capacity at Monument Lane, Birmingham (3E) until 1959 when he gained promotion to shedmaster at Bushbury (Wolverhampton), code 3B. This depot was to close to steam traction in 1963, Frank moving on as shedmaster to Aston, Birmingham (3D) for a short time until that depot's closure in 1964. With the demise of steam traction in the West Midlands area, he then moved to Tyseley, Birmingham as a fitter supervisor on the new diesel traction, retiring due to ill health in 1976.

These notes relate to his Ryecroft days when the railway companies attained maximum working flexibility from its employees among the artisan staff, for a wage that could be described as slightly above average for a working man during the Depression years. Frank soon learned as he progressed through his fitter's practical education, that a fitter was not solely required to maintain and repair the steam locomotive fleet at the shed, but also had to be available to repair and service the many and varied railway-owned installations within the shed's area – anything from water columns to goods yard cranes. One such area of maintenance covered by Ryecroft was a considerable way from the smoky hustle and bustle at the shed, being at Lichfield about 10 miles away. This was a task welcomed in summer, but in winter it could be viciously cold and exposed to all that season's elements. In L&NWR days the company had installed water hydraulic lifts at Lichfield City and Trent Valley stations. These required constant maintenance on a weekly basis, and also at other times due to emergency. The company made good use of the prevailing geology of the Lichfield area. Handily situated was the Ogley Hay to Huddlesford canal at Pipe Hill, approximately 1.5 miles from Lichfield City station. The elevation at Pipe Hill enabled water to flow via a pipeline situated along the railway line at Fosse Way level crossing, the fall allowing sufficient pressure to enable the lifts to operate succesfully. The system worked well but its Achilles heel was a lack of water pressure, often caused by blockage of the inlet grating by infiltration of floating weeds and waterside vegetation during the summer months. This would be added to by a wide variety of more substantial flotsam that found its way into the canal system. In severe winter conditions, of course, ice would be the principal problem of blocking the water flow, thus putting the station lifts out of service. The company built a fogman's hut near the intake, complete with coal supply facilities and a brazier. A daily visit by a permanent way lengthman kept a check on intake efficiency, with suitable ice-breaking tools kept in readiness in the hut together with the necessary supply of coal.

The fitter bound for Pipe Hill summit would board the footplate of a Bescot to Wychnor Junction freight train that was allowed to stop by pre-arrangement at Ryecroft Shed, where the operative and his heavy tool bag travelled in style to his destination. The fitter often solved the footplate staff's minor loco problems, and in return were sometimes allowed to do a bit of firing. On completion of the clearance of the inlet grating, came the mile-long walk along the track to Lichfiield City station where any other maintenance, such as replacing worn rubber washers, was undertaken. This would be completed by about midday when lunch was taken at the station staff's messroom. After a bit of convivial company and banter came a further mile-march to Trent Valley for routine checking and any needed maintenance to their lifts. These duties would be timed to be finished so as to coincide with a return to Walsall 'on the cushions' via a late afternoon Derby–Walsall local train, followed by a walk back to Ryecroft shed. As Frank Rigby related, 'a good job on a summer's day, but in vile winter conditions a purgatory and endurance much despised'. At least the job provided a safe haven from the attentions of the Ryecroft pranksters, whose high-spirited creativity could be triggered quickly on some unsuspecting recipient, with no one immune. Lightning could certainly, and devastatingly, strike the same place twice – but all in good humour at this lively shed.

Sid Hadley

Sid Hadley started his railway career in 1916 as a cleaner at Ryecroft and lived at 27, Lewis Street, Walsall, until he was almost ninety. His job on the L&NWR was obtained due to a personal recommendation to management by his next-door neighbour Billy Poullock, a top-link driver who started work at Ryecroft when the shed opened in 1877. On his promotion to fireman at the age of eighteen, Sid was served notice to report on a temporary transfer to Monument Lane shed, Birmingham, until their severe staff shortage was eased.

His duties were as a fireman on the New Street Station pilots. Theoretically, a three-shift system operated, but more typically it was a twelve-hour turn and sometimes for seven days a week. His was a humdrum job firing on the Webb 0-6-2 tank engines (known as 'gadgets'), most of the activity being attaching and detaching coaches and vans for the never-ending procession of express services calling at New Street. A lot of time was spent passing up and down the steep, smoke-filled tunnel from New Street to the fresh air at Monument Lane station and sidings. This included banking heavily loaded long-distance trains to the north, to avoid locomotives slipping to a standstill in the damp sulphurous conditions inside the tunnel. If this were to happen some highly complex manoeuvres to provide emergency assistance would have been required, which could have paralysed such a busy station. New Street was actually run as two stations, L&NWR and Midland. It was sometimes easier at busy times for the Webb tanks to cross over on to foreign metals to assist a stalled Midland engine. One such occasion saw Sid and his driver being called to the aid of a Midland Johnson single wheeler working a medium-weight express forward to Bristol. This was in the unfortunate and totally embarrassing nightmare of all drivers, being caught firmly in top dead centre, unable to move in either forward or reverse gear. The Monument Lane locomotive was crossed to Midland to provide the inertia to release the stranded Johnson from its incapacitating position. This enabled the L&NWR crew to enjoy some leg pulling of their rival Midland comrades, whose Derby bosses 'couldn't afford an extra pair of wheels and a coupling rod'. This was well and truly rubbed in by reminding the opposition that even L&NWR shunting engines had six wheels for adhesion and asking would they like to buy a pair?!

After a few months on the New Street pilot duties, Sid was allocated to the Albion shunt, a twenty-four-hour three-shift job based at the Albion canal interchange dock between Dudley Port and Smethwick. The Albion shunt locomotive left Monument Lane early on Monday morning and returned late on Saturday afternoon, after a complicated weeks activity. The 0-6-0 coal engine not only shunted the interchange basin but took in a mainline foray daily. Sid recalled that the shunt was always busy with boatloads of galvanised household products and galvanised sheets pouring in from the many canal side Black Country factories. These products were then transhipped into railway wagons for destinations in all parts of the United Kingdom, including ports for export abroad and throughout the Empire. When the shunt was finished, the coal engine worked a daily, circular pick-up freight to Bescot via Soho and Perry Barr Junctions. Wagons were attached and dropped off at small factory sidings and goods yards en route. On arrival at Bescot 'down' sidings, the loco left its trucks and vans to pick up another formation to return to Albion via Wednesbury and the Bloomfield curve, Tipton, and on to Albion. On arrival back at Albion, the night shift took over. This was the easiest shift of the three, but the night fireman (sometimes Sid) had to replenish the tender coal supply by shovel from conveniently placed wagons, to remove the necessity for a daily return to shed.

On the early shift starting at 6 a.m., a daily ritual was enacted at 9 a.m. From the direction of Brades Village, a well dressed affluent gentleman approached Albion station level crossing, riding a large, immaculately groomed white horse. This was Mr Stringer, the owner of several 'slave factories' around the Greets Green area, noted for their long hours and very poor pay.

Sid Hadley went 'foreign' for three years, firing on the Albion shunt. He was then recalled to Ryecroft shortly before the 1923 grouping, and saw the birth of the London Midland and Scottish Railway. The closure of Pleck New Mills Midland shed brought about an influx of Midland men to Bescot and Ryecroft, and Sid in his early twenties was fortunate to remain on the footplate. Throughout the Depression years he remained at Ryecroft, despite many of the shed's firemen being posted away to work at distant sheds on the LMS system. He did, however, have to work from Bescot at times, especially for the winter surges in coal transportation. During the 1930s Sid fired on all Ryecroft's links, including the elite duty, the Class A express freight to Camden Town. He also fired on the summer seaside traffic to Blackpool and the North Wales coast, earning the necessary 'overtime' helping to enlarge the pay packet.

Just prior to 1939, the railway was beginning to face real competition from the motor coach and private car, but the outbreak of hostilities brought terrific pressure on the great steel way. Passing out with several of his mates in their thirties, Sid became a driver to be put in a reserved occupation of national importance, working long hours with little time off. Some double turns extended to a full twenty-four hours. Perhaps the ultimate to be asked of footplate men was in the winter of 1940, when terrific snowfalls completely blocked the Cannock line for five days. A number of locomotives were engulfed by huge drifts in freezing and extreme weather. Sid was stranded on the footplate for eighteen hours on one day of this big freeze, these conditions being repeated in 1947.

In 1948 Sid Hadley was working for his third employer, as British Railways was established, and was still driving in 1957 as Ryecroft closed to steam operations. Months earlier, Sid and other Ryecroft drivers trained and were passed to drive the new diesel multiple units now based at Ryecroft, expected to revolutionise local passenger services. Alas, by 1960 many people became owners of a motor car, while improved bus services offering cheaper fares, resulted in fewer passengers and, consequently, loss of railway revenue. In the early 1960s, the Beeching axe fell on many local services operated by Ryecroft, the exception being the remunerative Walsall–Birmingham operation; of course now electrified and thriving.

Sid Hadley's swansong came on 17 January 1965, when he drove the last passenger diesel multiple unit train along the Cannock line, from Rugeley to New Street. He retired from railway service the following April. In retirement, Sid returned to the steam footplate on the Severn Valley Railway, often driving Stanier Class 5 mixed traffic 4-6-0 No.45110. Approaching seventy years of age, he decided to call it a day and retire. The Severn Valley Railway, having grown in strength, had produced a well-trained younger footplate staff. On another front, however, there was considerable pressure to reopen the Cannock line passenger service to Hednesford, and this resulted in a pleasant surprise for the Ryecroft veteran in 1986. A special diesel multiple unit was to run, to take British Rail officials and Walsall and Staffordshire councillors from Walsall to Hednesford, as part of a feasibility study for reopening the line. Sid Hadley, then eighty-five, was kindly and generously invited to ride once again on his familiar line. In 1989 permission was granted to reinstate the passenger service over the line, which was in good shape and regularly witnessing the passage of trains of over 1,000 tons of pulverised coal for Rugeley 'B' Power Station. Sid was once again to be a cab guest on a further trial run in January 1989. The retired driver

Diesel train run prior to reopening of the Cannock route to passenger trains with guest driver Sid Hadley, who had driven the last Cannock train in 1965, seen at Walsall station with railway managers and local councillors about to embark. (Jack Haddock Collection)

was ecstatic to hear that the first official passenger services would commence on Monday 10 April that year; the Phoenix had at last arisen at last from the ashes. Sid was yet again invited to a footplate trip on the official special train to reopen the line. This was scheduled to run from Birmingham to Hednesford on the morning of Friday 7 April 1989. Sid, unfortunately, was too ill to accept this second ride and he passed away two days later.

Ted Everton Ryecroft, 1900 to 1945

In whatever field of activity you might care to examine, there have always been a few men who have stood out from the rest in their manners, ways and personalities. Words to describe such men range from bubbly through extrovert to eccentric. They need not be brash and overpowering or domineering. They are not unkind or self centred, but their personalities proclaim them as different. You will find them on the street, in a club or on a factory floor, in fact anywhere. It seems the railway fraternity certainly had many of these people which we simply call 'characters'.

Ryecroft shed had many characters on its books over the years. One, Teddy Everton, was Ryecroft-based between 1900 and 1945. His obvious nickname 'Toffee', derived from the Merseyside confectionery. At this time Everton Football Club were known as the 'Toffee Men' for the same reason. Ted started work for the L&NWR as a cleaner, his railway service being broken as he was an early volunteer for wartime service at the outbreak of the First World War. Spending four years in the 5th Battalion of the South Staffordshire Regiment, he returned to Ryecroft in 1919. Ted was single at this time, and lived with parents at Walsall Arboretum lodge as his father was a park superintendent.

He did not sever his connections with the army, subsequently joining the South Staffs Territorials. While in the army he developed a fondness for a glass of ale, and better still, two. One must not get the impression he was a habitual drinker – he was not. But no matter how much he consumed, it seemed he was incapable of getting drunk.

Ted's wartime service saw him posted to the Middle East as Quartermaster Sergeant in charge of stores, including consumables for the 5th Battalion arriving by boat at Alexandria. Supervising the unloading of a cargo ship, and checking off the vast number of crates in the hold, his roving eye found two labelled as 'beer' for the sergeant's mess; and a further two containing wine and spirits for the officers. Of course the labelling was incorrect, and had to be amended. Teddy and his fellow sergeants were to have a very good night. The hard stuff was soon made non-recoverable and untraceable.

Ted's army life had considerably sharpened his humour, his repertoire being put to good use at Ryecroft, where there had long been a reputation of practical jokes among the staff. Ranging from the ridiculous to the almost dangerous, it was the young cleaners who suffered most. One young call-up lad was sent to knock-up Ted at the Arboretum lodge one morning, just before daybreak. Ted, ready for work, made the lad a cup of tea and the youngster asked about the possibility of acquiring a few duck eggs from the nests among the bushy islands of the ornamental lake. When Ted offered to row him out in one of the park's boats, the youth accepted with great enthusiasm. As the lad's shadowy form disappeared in the morning gloom, Ted rowed back to the boathouse and set off to the shed for duty. That was the day the Ryecroft call-up lad went missing, overdue and presumed lost. His eventual return caused a riot of mirth.

In 1925 Teddy Everton got married, left home and rented a small house in Whittimere Street, next door to the South Staffs Regimental barracks. Obviously the move had been carefully planned to allow him to act as caretaker and, more importantly, he became bar superintendent with access to all keys in the barracks. A deputy would undertake his duties when he was on unsociable shifts. One hot summer evening, Ted was firing to driver Fred Richardson on one of Ryecroft's top-link duties, the return Camden to Walsall Bodleys Long Street goods express freight. The loco was 5600 *Prince of Wales*, a L&NWR 4-6-0 renowned for its coal appetite and intense footplate heat, which developed a killer thirst. On the long run north with fifty wagons, several cans of tea were brewed and bottled water drunk (they were well prepared), but they both arrived to sign off with a raging thirst. Their routes home followed the same general direction along Hatherton Street. It was about 4 a.m. and Fred was about to continue to Caldmore (pronounced 'Karmer'), when Teddy's key came out and his mate was invited to a very unexpected pint. The long hot night had taken its toll. By 5.30 a.m. a merry Fred, who had downed a few, was walking home to Camden Street (a very strange coincidence) to be confronted by a policeman on Walsall Bridge awaiting his 6 a.m. relief. The constable thought he was seeing things, a rolling railwayman lurching across the bridge in overalls carrying his wicker luncheon basket and billycan. Fortunately the constable saw the funny side, and Fred Richardson continued along his way after a mild reprimand and a warning.

In 1930, on an evening in late January, the South Staffs Regiment held its annual dinner in its Walsall headquarters in Whittimere Street. Various local dignitaries and officials were always invited, including the Walsall stationmaster and the then Ryecroft shed superintendant, Mr John Waddington The latter was Teddy Everton's boss. After dinner and usual speeches, the focal point for several hours was the bar tended by the Ryecroft driver. He was being handsomely treated to several beers, and caught the sight of Mr Waddington's eye. He was a man of resolute habits, who drank in moderation. Knowing Teddy was due to sign on at 6 a.m., the shed chief left with his driver still sinking his ale; it was now about 2 a.m. Leading by example, Mr Waddington was an early riser and, expecting Teddy to be incapable of turn-out, went to the shed before 6 a.m. ready to detail one of the stand-by links to undertake Everton's duty. Teddy dutifully arrived on time, however, walking down the path from Mill Lane to the shed as straight as a die, clean shaven and dressed neatly in clean pressed overalls, carrying his tin snap box. 'Good morning Mr Waddington', said Ted, having the compliment returned. Mr Waddington watched Ted examine the notice board and then followed fireman and driver to the allotted Webb 2-4-2T No.6689, watching them climb aboard. By this time Mr Waddington had come to the conclusion that 'Toffee' was fit to do his driving duty in spite of the drinking spree witnessed earlier. As Ted was about to reverse 6689 into the yard for final check and oiling, the shedmaster asked him, 'Tell me Mr Everton, what is your limit in consuming ale?'. A short silence prevailed before the driver answered, 'I'm sorry sir, I don't know. I have had neither the time nor the money to put it to the test'. Ted opened the regulator to drift away out of the shed, leaving behind a very puzzled and speechless gaffer.

In steam days, the raucous call of a locomotive steam whistle was used in warning as express trains passed through stations at speed. The smaller shunting engines working round the clock in busy yards breaking and making up trains, similarly voiced the air with differing whistles. These were often codes between engine driver and signalman, guards and shunters. Railwaymen understood these whistles of communication, the general public being unaware of the complexity of what they were hearing. Teddy Everton had a whistle code of his own, an unmistakeable sound signature that stated personal presence, as a dog does with its scent. One of the most popular Ryecroft duties was the morning Walsall to Derby local, crews in the link undertaking this duty as part of a six-weekly rota. Starting at about 11 a.m., the duty finished at 8 p.m., leaving plenty of time for a drink. When Ted was on the job, the distinctive whistle pattern triggered a response at Pelsall station on the down trip. A one-minute stop was allowed for passengers to alight and embark, the whistle sounding not for railway purposes, but to alert the landlord of the hotel conveniently situated next to the station. As the train pulled in at 12.12 p.m., the driver scampered the few steps, correct money in hand, to collect a full pint already drawn, handle facing the door. The glass would be drained, (railwaymen maintaining that the liquid never touched the sides of their throats), then a quick exit by-passing the ticket collector who knew the routine, to join the footplate for the 12.13 p.m. departure and the guard's green flag. Soon the train was accelerating away, with the loco's water tanks still almost full and Teddy's registering less than half. Of course, alcohol consumption on duty was an offence.

With the drill hall on one side of Teddy's Whittimere Street home, his neighbour on the other side was a much respected constable of the Walsall Police Force, PC Ayres. Friday in the 1930s was payday, and welcomed by both police and railway staff after their week's toil. The wage packet was signed for and handed over between 12 and 1 p.m. With no smoke

Ryecroft shed's Webb 0-6-0 'Caulilower' 28597 working a Birmingham to Rugeley local at Bescot station, 1936. (Harry Rusell)

limitations in force back then, almost every household was heated by coal, and chimneys had to be regularly swept to limit the possibility of chimney fires, then an offence. The cost of a professional sweep was about *2s 6d*, a large amount from the limited wages of the Depression years, so many households deliberately fired their chimneys to save money. With a possible Fire Brigade call-out and wasting of that department's time, the police summoned proven offenders, who had to attend court. Knowing the concentration of police at the Goodall Street Police station for the payroll hour, Friday was not only Freya's day, but also fires day. However, some policemen did remain on duty as Teddy Everton found out. He had been on night duty and after snatching a few hours' sleep, rose in time to visit Ryecroft to pick up his pay and, being a dutiful husband, left a well-stoked-up fire. Leaving Whittimere Street he crossed Lichfield Street to walk along Hatherton Road, and for some unknown reason he turned to look behind, and saw dense clouds of smoke being emitted by his chimney. He decided to ignore it, and turned to continue to Ryecroft to view a young policeman coming towards him eying the pall of smoke. Ted had visions of a summons, the usual report in the press and the subsequent ribald laughter from his mates at the shed. Knowing the constable was walking quicker now, obviously intent on an arrest, Teddy decided to take the initiative and literally stopped the officer in his tracks to ask if he knew who the offending householder might be. The constable seemed pleased with the offered assistance. 'Whose house is it then ?', the policeman enquired, 'It will be an interesting court case'. Ted responded, 'It happens to be my neighbour, a member of your force, the jocular PC Ayres'. With that comment from a very straight-faced Teddy, the constable decided he had never seen the incident and beat a hasty retreat. Looking round to see if a sergeant was in sight, the young constable headed up a side road to the Butts district to seek anonymity and sanctuary, leaving Ted with a broad grin on his face and feeling very self satisfied with the outcome of his chimney cleaning endeavour.

Ted passed away in 1956. He had often wished he could return to the footplate and the work he loved. More importantly, he missed his mates and the camaraderie of Ryecroft shed. Ted could dish it out, but true to Ryecroft form, he was 'suckered' by his mates intent on letting him know that Ryecroft humour was never one-sided. No one was immune to a vicious counter-attack in a least expected moment. 'All for one and one for all.'

The Country Lad who Tamed Simeon Foster

This true story recounts the footplate happenings of a summer Walsall to Blackpool excursion, aboard 'Experiment' 4-6-0 5506 *Lord of The Isles*, driven by the redoubtable Simeon Foster of Ryecroft shed. Simeon had the reputation of almost single handedly being responsible for writing off 3C's time-expired 'Experiments' and 'Prince of Wales' 4-6-0s to the scrapyard. Incidentally, it was much to the favour of Ryecroft's fitting staff. Simeon was one of several heavy-handed drivers who helped these Whale & Bowen Cooke (both chief mechanical engineers to the L&NWR) products to oblivion. His driving methods probably helped the LMS Board of Directors to appoint William A. Stanier as CME, leading to the provision of more durable and efficient locomotive classes to cope with the increasing tonnage of freight and passenger trains in the pre-Second World War era.

Firing for the likes of Simeon for a day was near purgatory. Many young firemen have been known to exchange turns in order to avoid being rostered to fire for the forceful driver, but there was, of course, always someone willing and able to operate the shovel for a day to the seaside. During the slump years of the 1930s, a Sunday Blackpool trip was financially very rewarding, adding 10 to 15*s* to a fireman's weekly pay. Sometime after Tommy Bates had suffered as a consequence of full open regulator thrashing of *Ethelred* to Blackpool, the fireman assigned to *Lord of The Isles* was Colin Mould. Colin was not a local man but came from the country district of Uttoxeter, being born and bred of healthy farming stock. He was a superb physical specimen, muscular and 6ft tall, and weighing about 15 stone. Reputations or none, firing for Simeon held no fears for the younger man.

No.5506 *Lord of The Isles* had been taken off mainline express duties and allocated to Ryecroft in the twilight years of its working life, where its duties could be considered to be of a less demanding nature. The pair booked on just before 7 a.m. and set about preparing the 'Lord' for the road, Colin noting carefully the huge pile of stacked coal on the tender. Theoretically, this was enough to achieve a return to Walsall without the need to resort to the Blackpool coaler, thus helping to avoid congestion at Blackpool North shed. At about 7.15 a.m. they left Ryecroft to run light engine to pick up the stock for their excursion, timed to depart from Walsall's platform 2 at 8.45 a.m.

The day proved warm and sunny and, consequently, the train was very popular, filled to capacity with many passengers standing. *Lord of The Isles* left the station with a spectacularly noisy fireworks display, the hard-pressed 4-6-0 slipping violently several times before No.1 signal box was reached. On joining the old Grand Junction mainline at Darlaston, Simeon began thrashing the ageing 'Experiment' while Colin kept hard at it on the shovel. After several sharp sprints followed by the usual checks expected on a summertime Blackpool job, *Lord of The Isles* passed through Preston as it was approaching midday, to join the queue of excursion trains nearing Kirkham Junction. Colin noted that the tender's coal content had become somewhat depleted and was, in fact, approaching half empty. Coaling at Blackpool was only to be undertaken in dire emergency, as one locomotive working out of a very tight servicing timetable at a shed dealing with about 100 visiting locomotives, could produce chaos.

Colin Mould decided he had enough coal to return to Ryecroft unless delays or diversions on the return trip occurred. The thought passed through the fireman's mind that there was possibly a chance that Simeon Foster would ignore the coal supply and drive home regardless of any economy needed. His driver did not discuss the situation with Colin, who, nevertheless, had decided what to do if any opportunity arose. Having a great sense of humour, Colin eagerly awaited payback time. After the afternoon of rest, which normally included a gentle stroll along the promenade; watching the trams and horsedrawn Landaus; taking in the seascape, the bathers and the pleasure boats; it was time to rejoin their mount on North shed. They gently coupled up to their stock at platform 10 of Talbot Road station, after their usual preparation and oiling routines. Most of the platforms were filled with trains returning home via Preston, so congestion and delayed running was to be encountered, but strangely no further empty stock trains were being propelled into the station's vacant platforms. On normal summer weekends from about 6 p.m. to midnight, as soon as one train left, empty stock for a later departure followed quickly into the vacant platform. Inactivity spelt trouble!

With the clock showing time for the Walsall excursion to depart, a station inspector boarded the footplate to inform Simeon Foster that a points failure had occurred by Preston signal box, affecting Blackpool traffic running onto the West Coast mainline. It had been repaired in a short time, but the driver would encounter a tail back of trains before clearing Preston. Right of way was given and *Lord of The Isles* made a spirited start, the driver optimistically hoping that the backlog would be cleared quickly to enable a clear run to Preston. However, on this particular evening the failure produced far-reaching knock-on effects, including services on the mainline. With timetabled West Coast Mainline expresses having priority, they found on eventually reaching Preston that their critical pathing between up expresses had been lost, and they were routed mainly up the slow lines in the four-track sections to Crewe. This was reached one hour late, by which time Colin was bringing coal from the rear of the tender. His driver was given the 'up fast' from Crewe, the regulator was opened and the locomotive was worked at full bore. He was totally concentrating on his driving and completely oblivious of Colin's problem of an almost empty tender.

Foster was in his element, living up to his nickname of 'Major Seagrave', emulating his motor racing hero. The tired old 'Experiment' was being thrashed to the limit with cinders and red-hot char blasting skywards into the dark evening sky. A clear road was given through Stafford and Simeon on passing Queensville Junction, blissfully pressed on to Wolverhampton. Colin's plan was working. The timing was immaculate, conceived to give Simeon a shock and teach him a lesson not to ignore the problems of a fireman struggling with a locomotive that had seen better days, but also schemed not to cause any trouble with the local locomotive inspector. Approaching Penkridge, only a few shovelfuls were left in the tender. *Lord of The Isles* would not reach Walsall. It would be degrading, a crime, to fail in section out of steam and coal. Passing Gailey, Colin looked at the pressure gauge at 60mph – pressure was good. Next he looked at Simeon Foster's back, hand on the fully open regulator, his eyes intent on the road as the ballast flashed by. After a pause, Colin tapped his shoulder and shouted in his ear, 'Sim lad, I've finished work, it's the first time I've finished work on the footplate before the driver'. 'What do you mean', retorted Simeon, surprised. Colin, with a crestfallen look, pointed to the empty tender and said, 'A fireman cannot work without coal'. Simeon looked at his mate, swore at him good naturedly and realised he was a victim of opportunity. 'Alright Colin, you've had your joke. I'll stop at Four Ashes box for you to drop off and inform the signalman to tell Fordhouses box to route us via the "up goods loop" at Bushbury sidings, so we can detach the train and get coal from 3B.'

As *Lord of The Isles* came to a halt outside Four Ashes box, the signalman was already looking from the window with a premonition of trouble to affect his tight, busy traffic margins. Colin hastened up the steps of the typical L&NWR box and a sympathetic signalman made the necessary calls to solve Simeon's dilemma. On arrival at Bushbury, the alerted shed turners had prepared a road to the coaling plant. Emergencies such as this had happened before; to them it was a routine procedure.

By the time the 'Experiment' had run onto the shed the steam pressure was falling. It took about 15 minutes to go on shed, coal and return to the train. Colin was busy firing in order to pull the boiler round to the required 175lb per square inch working pressure, as Simeon looked on encouragingly. After the enforced delay, *Lord of The Isles* was reunited with its train load of tired daytrippers. Bushbury No.1 immediately found a road for the excursion to return to Walsall, via the Grand Junction link. Walsall was quickly reached and the passengers detrained. A station inspector came up to Simeon to inform him to uncouple the flogged 'Experiment' and to proceed to Ryecroft shed. Control had been informed of the Bushbury emergency and arrangements had been made for a relieving locomotive to take the empty stock back to North Junction sidings, for further storage. Already waiting in platform 1a (the 'Cannock' bay) was 0-6-0 3333, an ex-Midland Class 3F of Ryecroft shed. On depositing the old 4-6-0 on the Ryecroft disposal road, Simeon went to the office to make out the usual routine report and handed it to the shed's running foreman. The officer, knowing of the coal-eating propensity of the type, informed him that no action would be taken regarding his stopping the train in section to acquire coal at Bushbury. Evidently, the old thoroughbred had been earmarked to be quickly withdrawn, to be replaced by a more modern and fuel-efficient 'Prince of Wales' 4-6-0 for mixed traffic duties. The foreman was not to know that if Colin Mould had decided to inform his driver of the suspect coal situation, this emergency could have been avoided. However, it was Colin Mould's hour of glory. His plan to shock the shed's most heavy-handed driver was soon known around Ryecroft shed, and was greeted with great mirth and hilarity. Colin himself became a driver, and one that did not hang about either. Having been apprenticed to the master, something would undoubtedly have been expected to rub off. Ryecroft's staff was only human after all.

Above: Ryecroft shed staff, *c.*1928. (Jack Haddock Collection)

Left: Ryecroft shed staff, *c.*1930. (Jack Haddock Collection)

Tommy Bates, Sins of the Fathers

A fine July morning in 1932 found a young LMS Walsall Ryecroft Shed fireman named Tommy Bates walking through the Ryecroft streets at the early hour of 5.30 a.m. Due to book on duty at 5.45 a.m., he found the freshness of the slightly cool air exhilarating; passing public houses, the smell of stale beer was the only reminder of the previous long hot day of the heatwave. He was booked for a Walsall to Blackpool North day excursion. Thinking of his forthcoming task, he knew that when the sun rose higher and the temperature rose with it, he would be on the footplate working virtually a double trip to Blackpool – the down run between the hours of 7.30 a.m. and booking-off at Blackpool North Shed approximately at 1.30 p.m.; the up run departing Blackpool North about 7.30 p.m., arriving at Walsall around midnight, but because of congestion on the road, this time was seldom achieved. Most firemen and drivers on Blackpool excursions took advantage of using the old rolling stock at Blackpool North shed, converted to sleeping compartments, for rest before the gruelling return trip.

Coming over Mill Street railway bridge, Tommy Bates viewed the Sunday congestion of smoking locomotives on the outside links of Ryecroft shed, wondering which steed he would be wrestling with until after dinner time. Lined up were 'Prince of Wales' Class locomotives alongside 'Experiments', 'George the Fifths', 'Midland Compounds' and 'Class Twos'. All the ex-L&NWR engines being notorious fire eaters, Tommy knew what to expect. Cautiously wending his (illegal) way over the Cannock line, he walked down the shed, passing the dead local shunting and freight engines at rest for the Sabbath. Perusing the notice board, he noted that his engine was 'Experiment' Class 4-6-0 No.5504 *Ethelred*. This, together with the fact that the previous evening he had been allocated to fire for Simeon Foster, caused him to wince at the thought of his combination of locomotive and driver.

Tommy Bates's problem was that the 'Experiment' locomotives allocated to Ryecroft shed had seen better days, and were now approaching their time for the scrap heap. After many years on mainline work, small local sheds had acquired them for secondary duties and, subsequently, they were in run-down condition. This made them notorious fire eaters and rough riders on long trips, not a thought to be relished on the 240-mile trip to Blackpool and back. The second problem for Tommy was his driver. Here one must explain that driver Foster was an extremely popular and well-liked driver at Ryecroft, the shed being known to many outside railwaymen as a 'Happy shed', practical jokes being a regular part of Ryecroft life. The fact was, like many former L&NWR drivers, Simeon Foster had a fixation that the only way to get the best out of any locomotive was to drive with the regulator fully open, and literally thrash it as hard as possible between points A and B. Time must be kept at all costs, and if possible time was to be saved. It was acknowledged that Foster was the hardest and most exasperating driver for any young Ryecroft firemen to serve. Upon him was bestowed the nickname 'Major Seagrave', after the famous road motor-racing star of the halcyon days of the 1930s.

On this particular day Tommy Bates drew his tools and equipment from the stores and proceeded to the footplate of *Ethelred*. The locomotive had been prepared by the shed turners and was fully loaded with a maximum coal capacity of 10 tons, ten hundredweight carefully stacked just above tender height. Because of traffic congestion on Blackpool North shed, most locomotives had to make a round trip without re-coaling. Presently,

Ex-LNWR Experiment Class loco 25504 *Ethelred* in LMS livery, shunting at Walsall's ex-Midland railway carriage sidings, *c*.1928. (W.A. Camwell)

Simeon Foster joined Tommy on the footplate, and *Ethelred* began to move slowly among the row of smoking excursion locomotives down to the ringing-off hut. Permission to leave shed was immediately granted by Ryecroft signal box, the small 'Tommy Dodd' (ground) signal indicating right of way. *Ethelred* drifted off shed, down the cutting and through the station to the Midland yard carriage sidings, using a spare road to the New Mills bridge end of the sidings. Immediately a train of ten corridor coaches was propelled from the Midland yard goods sidings by the small ex-Midland Railway shunter No.1690, affectionately known as *Jacko*, onto the waiting *Ethelred*.

With the departure of *Jacko* back to its goods sidings, Walsall No.1 signal box had prepared a road in liason with Walsall No.2 and *Ethelred* propelled its train down onto No.2 Platform at Walsall station. This movement was carried out with usual railway efficiency in the minimum of time. From the point of arriving in Walsall station and the mad scramble of passengers for seats, Tommy Bates's agony had begun. With a clear road by Bodleys and Pleck Junction signal boxes, Simeon Foster slowly notched up the regulator wide, whereupon Tommy began his stint with the shovel. By Portobello Junction, *Ethelred* was moving at a good 60mph, with only a small cut-off. This meant Tommy being continuously at the shovel, except for the odd few moments. Glancing out of the cab he viewed the sky – not a cloud in sight; the heat wave was obviously still in evidence. As the excursion clattered over Bushbury Junction, Simeon blasted the whistle, probably to let the Bushbury shed men in sight know that Ryecroft men also knew how to work fast trains. On to Stafford *Ethelred* continued flat out, rocking, lurching and vibrating along the track. Here one can only ponder the inequality of human endeavour. On this train of some 500 people, including many children, sat all the passengers having not a care in the world, idly viewing the rural landscape with its grazing cattle and town backstreets. Most of them would be engaged in casual gossip, together with their yelling, excited children absorbing quantities of sweets and bottles of pop. Of the two men on the footplate, the driver was having the grave responsibility for their safety, accompanied by his poor fireman, working his fingers to the bone.

By the time Stafford had been passed, the sun was rising higher to add to the footplate discomfort. Beyond Stafford to Crewe, the tracks became quadrupled. *Ethelred* was allocated the 'down' slow line. Presently, a northbound express was pulled alongside on the 'down' fast fine by 'Royal Scot' Class locomotive No.6111, *Royal Fusilier.* Simeon's answer to this challenge was to try and coax even more speed out of the already extended output of *Ethelred. Royal Fusilier,* however, gradually outpaced the seaside excursion. It must have been quite a sight from the coaches of the northbound express with steam emitting from various joints in the 'Experiment', together with the volume of sparks and char blasting skywards from the chimney. Meanwhile, Tommy Bates just fired away mechanically into the insatiable *Ethelred*'s firebox. He found time for a quick drink of cold tea from a pop bottle while slowly running through the maze of the Crewe Junction network. Firing not being required, he had to assist Simeon Foster concentrating on the many complicated signal patterns. After the Crewe slack, *Ethelred* was soon gathering speed towards Weaver Junction. Heavy firing, corresponding with the sun's increasing heat, made footplate life very uncomfortable. About 11.45 a.m., after a number of distant-signal checks around Warrington and Wigan, Preston station was reached. Coming to a dead stand here, *Ethelred*'s was only one of the very many Blackpool excursions filtering down the Fylde Coast lines (all signal boxes to Kirkham and Wesham were fully occupied for short section working). *Ethelred* finally got right of way, and proceeded on a stop-start routine all the way on to Blackpool North, Talbot Road excursion sidings, taking about an hour to cover this last short stretch. Approaching Talbot Road, Tommy looked out of the cab towards the assembly of coaching stock and disgorging passengers. The sun was scorching and there was no wind whatever. On the footplate the heat was almost unbearable – even Simeon Foster was beginning to wilt, for on the way up he had been able to lean out of the cab for long periods to cool in the slipstream. Tommy got down to uncouple from the coaching stock to allow a local engine to draw away the stock for disposal.

With the numerous excursions to Talbot Road, within the eight hours until midday, most Ryecroft men wondered and marvelled at the disposal problem. Because of siding congestion, Blackpool excursion stock was filtered back along the line as far as Preston, Wigan, Southport and Blackburn, hauled by the useful ex-Lancashire & Yorkshire Railway 0-6-0 tender and 2-4-2 '2P' tank engines. Some five minutes after uncoupling, Tommy gave a sigh of relief as the coaching stock drew away. Almost immediately, the call-on signal cleared to run light engine out of North station. Blackpool shed confines were shortly reached, and Simeon Foster handed over *Ethelred* to the disposal men, who had the thankless task of cleaning the fireboxes of scores of locomotives in a mean temperature of about 88°F. Simeon and Tommy at first decided on a good cold-water wash before some snap. At this point it was common for any visiting train crew to visit

This is Tommy Bates who fired for driver Simeon Foster, seen at Ryecroft on loco 2745 used on the Class 1 freight Walsall to Camden. (Jack Haddock Collection)

Blackpool sands for a session in a deckchair. Alternatively, the men could get their heads down for a few hours in the specially converted old railway coaches with fitted bunks. Simeon and Tommy chose the latter, and somehow managed to get some sleep in the still baking-hot conditions. A call lad came into the coach around 6 p.m. to give Simeon and Tommy time to prepare *Ethelred* with full steam for the run back to Walsall, leaving Talbot Road excursion platforms at 7.48 p.m. He was just as apprehensive with regards to the return journey as he had been before the outward journey. Admittedly the sun was beginning to wane, but the continuing ridge of high pressure over England could only mean a warm, humid evening and night. Tommy knew he was in for another gruelling stint with his gleaming work shovel.

There was no hope of Simeon changing his driving methods, so Tommy just accepted his fate as *Ethelred* left Blackpool North shed and backed onto its waiting stock. Looking down the platform from the cab of *Ethelred*, Simeon and Tommy viewed their Walsall day trippers searching for empty compartments. Every child, it seemed, carried a bucket and spade and was, as usual, full of noise and, generally, laughter. Their fathers mostly appeared to have in their pockets a few bottles of ale, having realised it would be closing time when they reached Walsall. To go without a drink on a Sunday night was sheer torture to some. Of the mothers their expressions generally were, 'Oh I will be glad to get back home, having been up very early to get the children ready'. Considering their thankless task of damping down the children's spirits towards bedtime, and thinking of the Monday washing, one can appreciate the housewife's lot on a Sunday day excursion. With the train full, Simeon watched for the signal and, when cleared, slowly moved *Ethelred* away from Talbot Road to join in the usual stop-start procedure all the way back to Preston. Simeon was set to drive in his usual manner of continual thrashing, causing Tommy to fire just that bit harder than for other drivers, who preferred to ease and coax their locomotives along. It took about an hour to reach Preston, with anxious looks passing between footplate and signal cabins. After Preston, running along the slow lines, progress was improved. Passing Wigan and Warrington and other small towns, Simeon's heavy method of driving was responsible for cascading red-hot char and small lumps of coal skywards to descend into back gardens and rows of 'Coronation Street'-type houses. But the Lancastrians were used to this procedure and had long learned to live with the ex-L&NWR engines.

During a brief respite from shovelling, Tommy stole a few moments from his ordeal to take a drink of cold tea, again from the usual pop bottle, finding time to answer the waves of schoolchildren who were always in evidence with their notebooks full of engine numbers. On the approach to Crewe, signal checks began to put the Walsall excursion behind schedule. One good point was that night was drawing in, and Tommy was more than pleased to see his enemy the sun disappear below the horizon. Just after ten o'clock Ethelred was given a road through the Crewe bottleneck, by way of the up goods loop lines, bypassing the station under tunnels, and rejoining the up slow lines at Basford. Tommy Bates, shortly after leaving the Crewe lines, managed to put down the shovel for a chat with Simeon Foster. It was just before Norton Bridge Junction signal box, where the driver of an up train was required to whistle appropriately to the signalman for the road to Wolverhampton. This procedure was for the Norton Bridge signalman to inform the Stafford signal box responsible for working the Trent Valley and Stour Valley lines. Tommy reminded Simeon, because Simeon had been known to forget. Once he had been in charge of a Crewe to Curzon Street fish train and, having forgotten to whistle, was diverted along the Trent Valley line. Too late to rectify his mistake, the only alternative was to stop at the nearest signal box to ask for a road via Cannock and Walsall, causing some heavy graft for the poor fireman concerned on the Cannock Chase incline. In *Ethelred*'s case, Tommy had no illusions about firing this ageing 'Experiment' over that route. With the correct whistle given at Norton Bridge box, Simeon literally thrashed the rattling Ryecroft locomotive towards Stafford. By this time, Tommy was spending most of his time down the bottom end of the tender, facing the footplate end, throwing coal forward. Tommy viewed the cascade of sparks blasting upwards into the night sky, thinking that some drivers would work out a less demanding firing routine by skillfully adjusting cut-off and regulator openings. But not Simeon Foster. Just full bore and wide open regulator.

Eventually *Ethelred* rattled through Stafford station and Junction and on towards Wolverhampton, where Tommy checked his coal supply, and calculated that he could just about make Ryecroft shed with a few shovel fulls to spare. He had by then thrown nearly ten tons into *Ethelred*'s firebox. Among Ryecroft shedmen, it was common knowledge that Simeon had once completely emptied a tender on a previous Blackpool excursion around Four Ashes station, and had to call on Bushbury Shed for extra coal to get the last few miles to Walsall. Given a clear road to Bushbury Junction, *Ethelred* thrashed on, and

Tommy, almost dropping asleep, was firing purely by reflex action. Simeon still continued to emulate the legendary 'Major Seagrave', however, and from Bushbury and down the 'Old Road' *Ethelred* sped on, through Pleck Junction and eventually into Walsall No.1 platform at approximately 12.30 a.m. on the Monday. Bleary-eyed parents and still noisy children clattered their way up the curving steps to the L&NWR-style covered passage, leading into the concourse for tickets to be collected. The good news for Tommy was the arrival of an inspector, who instructed him to uncouple *Ethelred* from its stock and run light engine to Ryecroft shed. The stock was to be drawn into Midland Road carriage sidings in due course as available, by the yard shunter. So, with about two hundredweight of coal left in the tender, *Ethelred* retired to its home shed. Simeon Foster drove by the ringing-off hut, with its shed arrival bell ringing busily, and ran onto the disposal road behind another 'Experiment' and an engine of the 'Prince of Wales' Class, just in from similar excursions. The shed turner arrived to ask Simeon if *Ethelred* was still in one piece, knowing 'Sim's' way of thrashing the ex-mainline veterans.

Tommy wearily gathered up his snapbox and tools and proceeded to the booking-off office. Into the shed and down No.1 road he staggered with aching knees and arms. On reaching the bottom end of the shed he noticed, peeping through the dim gaslight and drifting smoke, a figure at the drinking water fountain, in the act of filling up the huge one-gallon iron kettle for the messroom firegrate. The figure was Simeon Foster's young son Les, working the night shift on calling up and messroom duties. Les Foster, who had joined the railway with the object of following in father's footsteps, became uncomfortably aware of Tommy leaning on his well-worn shovel and glaring in his direction with a look to kill. Suddenly, from the lips of Tommy Bates, there leapt an exclamation that was to live in the memories of Ryecroft shed staff until the present day:

> Young Les, it is said somewhere in the Bible that all sins of the parents shall be passed down to the first, second, third, and fourth generations, and so be it, that if I ever get you on the footplate as my fireman on a Blackpool excursion I shall make you suffer, sweat and toil in the same manner that your bloody old man has treated me today.

Tommy Bates tottered away to the toolroom stores, leaving a bewildered young Les Foster speechless. Considering that Tommy had not been to Sunday school for many years, it was amazing that in his mind still retained the learned text from the Bible, taken from the Second Commandment:

> I the Lord, am not easily angered, and I show great love and faithfullness, and forgive sin and rebellion, yet I will not fail to punish children and grandchildren to the third and fourth generations for the sins of their parents.

Fortunately, in the vicinity, overhearing this classic remark, were fitter Frank Rigby and fireman Walter Franklin, who found this confrontation most amusing. It took little or no time for the whole of Ryecroft shed staff to hear of this encounter, and they looked forward to the day in a few years time when Tommy Bates might have passed fireman Les Foster on the footplate with him. Alas, this true story has a sad ending.

Tommy became a very efficient fireman, and duly passed out on his examination to be a driver on Ryecroft Shed. On only his second week driving on one of the shunting links, he booked on duty one morning full of zest and enthusiasm for a day's work, when in the act of putting his snapbox on a high point on a 'Super D's' tender, he stood on the tender brake wheel to lift himself. Unfortunately, he slipped as the loose wheel revolved and fell awkwardly, hitting his head against the steel tender frame, to be killed almost instantaneously, and so never lived to carry out his threat to young Les Foster.

Tidman Masters

Tidman Masters started at Ryecroft as a cleaner in L&NWR days, eventually graduating to the position of driver, a post he held until his retirement from railway service just after the Second World War. With humour and conviviality the norm at the depot, Tidman never appreciated or instigated any of the practical jokes generated by his work mates. These pranks were often made to offset the long, unsociable hours and working conditions encountered at the shed. Variety at Walsall was the spice of life, the 'spice' often being hot, fast, ruthless and making its appearance in any guise at any time – often appearing unannounced, and with the intensity of a thunderbolt to the intended recipient. Tidman was more of an introvert who kept himself to himself, shunning social and sporting occasions, but was a very reliable and conscientious man. Few of his footplate companions relished a day's duty with him as he said little in conversation, his attention at all times firmly on the road and the performance of his mount, working efficiently by the rule book and widely respected by management as 100 per cent reliable.

One day in the 1930s, both management and staff had a surprise and shock when opening their daily newspapers. At that time, and over many years, the promotion of 'Bile Beans' featured as advertisements in the press. They emphasised the product's efficacy and value for keeping fit and healthy. 'Bile Beans keep you fit' not only appeared in printed form; the slogan also being seen in the sky above, in the shape of a banner towed by a Tiger Moth bi-plane or something similar. The papers running the advert at first chose well-known sportsmen and public figures to illustrate how the 'beans' kept them healthy and at peak fitness, to sustain their daily exertions. The firm's ad-men then focused on various occupations of the working man, with an interior page feature about 6x6in, which included a picture of the person at work, each advert running for approximately a month. The most popular daily newspaper of the 1930s was the *Daily Herald*, a moderate socialist publication that appealed to Labour Party supporters and was especially popular with railway and transportation staff of that era. With the emphasis on healthy living for the working man, the varied adverts featured a miner, followed by a stevedore, a navvy and then a bus driver. Everyone was expecting a railwayman, and one morning Ryecroft was amazed to see a photograph of Tidman Masters in contemplative mood, leaning out from the cab of a 3C Fowler 3P 2-6-2 tank locomotive. The caption stated, 'This driver keeps healthy and never loses time thanks to regularly taking his Bile Beans'. No one had ever seen Tidman taking 'Beans' while on duty, although, of course, he could have done so at home. The advert caused a stir at Ryecroft, which could not let the situation go unnoticed or without celebration. The plot was soon hatched.

45500 'Patriot' on shed turntable after working the Manchester to Walsall leg of the Pines Express, 1955. (Jack Haddock Collection)

On orders from the shed's acknowledged principal perpetrator of practical jokes, all staff with access to adverts were instructed to carefully cut them out of their newspapers, the final count running into several hundreds. Simultaneously, a quantity of the strongest glue was acquired from a local glue factory, which was dependent on one of Ryecroft's shunt duties for its delivery of cowhides. Tidman went unsuspecting about his duties in his usual quiet way. One early morning he reported for duty allocated to a Fowler 3P similar to the one in the advert. It was routine for a driver to prepare his own engine, so he drew his supply of tools and lubrication from the stores to join his fireman on his walk to the engine. A great shock awaited Tidman as he saw his charge literally festooned with hundreds of 'Bile Beans' adverts glued to the locomotive, especially on the side tanks. With no time to attempt a face-saving removal, he ran off shed to couple up to his stock in the carriage sidings, to work his early morning local. It was left to the elements and the heat from the locomotive to remove Ryecroft's massive patchwork.

Harry Cotterel

The late Harry Cotterel was a fitter at Ryecroft shed from 1906 to 1914. He left Ryecroft for war service and did not return, but chose to follow a railway career that took him to the Great Northern works at Doncaster, then to try his luck on railways in both North and South America. I visited him in his Bloxwich bungalow when he was over ninety years old. He had often had to attend to running repairs on 2158 *Sister Dora*, such as slight brake adjustments on its daily visit to Ryecroft shed. *Sister Dora* had a regular driver, a Mr Sayer of Burton-on-Trent, L&NWR shed, who was allocated to the small two road

This is the only known shot of a new Britannia Class loco 70052 testing Ryecroft's turntable in 1954. The photographer witnessed the problems of turning the loco with only inches to spare. Did it arrive on clearance test trials or was this a mistake? (David Spiers)

sub-shed at Derby. When Harry performed any repair to *Sister Dora* Sayer would watch him like a hawk and make sure the repairs were to his satisfaction. Sayer then went over the engine frame with his cleaning rag wiping off even fingermarks. Harry and others who knew Sayer say he was totally obsessed with *Sister Dora* and seemed to regard the engine as his personal property. On *Sister Dora*'s annual visits to Crewe for planned maintenance, Sayer did not relish driving a substitute engine. At no time from 1895 can anyone I have spoken to recall *Sister Dora* becoming a total failure.

Walter Franklin and 2158 Sister Dora

Walter Franklin, now aged eighty-nine, was a cleaner on Ryecroft shed just before the First World War. He started work at Ryecroft in 1912 and retired in 1960, having served the L&NWR, the London Midland & Scottish Railway, and finally British Railways. He well remembers *Sister Dora* arriving at midday with its regular driver named Mr Sayer, who was one of the old breed of Victorian railwaymen. He evidently preferred to have his 'snap' on the footplate of *Sister Dora*, instead of joining the lads in the Ryecroft mess room. When not eating or drinking his tea, Mr Sayer spent the rest of his spare time cleaning and oiling *Sister Dora* until it was time to take up his return duty to Derby. If any young Ryecroft shed lads wanted to board his engine or were in its vicinity, they were promptly ordered off.

At this point it is prudent to mention the reason why the mighty L&NWR named a locomotive after a Walsall nurse. In the Black Country town of Walsall on 28 December 1878, the funeral took place of Dorothy Pattison, known to every citizen of Walsall as Sister Dora. Born in Hauxwell, a small village in the North Riding of Yorkshire, on

The LNWR loco named after the nurse Dorothy Pattison who devoted her life to caring for Walsall's sick. A special relationship built up between Sister Dora, as she was known, and local railwaymen. (John Bucknall Collection)

16 January 1832, she arrived in Walsall on 8 January 1865. The bearers at her funeral consisted of eighteen railwaymen. These included engine drivers, porters and guards, all in working uniform. The procession took the route over Bodley's crossing to reach the cemetary at Queen Street, where her grave remains to this day. It appears that almost every citizen of Walsall attended this funeral, from the Mayor to the humble working class.

Sister Dora's time in Walsall coincided with a period of industrial growth when working conditions were, to say the least, somewhat primitive. Subsequently, accidents became a daily occurrence. Safety rules appertaining to machinery were almost non-existent. This applied particularly to the local railway system that was in a period of expansion. Railwaymen from all departments became prone to accidents, particularly severed limbs. With their frequent visits to the Walsall Bridge Street hospital, then the Cottage hospital in Bradford Street and the temporary Bridgeman Place hospital, rented from the L&NWR company during the smallpox epidemic, a special friendship evolved between Sister Dora and Walsall railwaymen. One afternoon in June 1873, Sister Dora was summoned to the front steps of the hospital to be confronted by a group of ailwaymen, immaculately dressed in their best off-duty suits, with flowers in their buttonholes. They presented her with a pony and carriage, paid for out of their own wages, at a cost of £50. Being a modest and independent person, she tried to refuse this gift, but with persuasion from the vicar of Walsall, it was ultimately put to good use for visiting the sick and outpatients.

From the Cottage hospital (the site of Walsall's now demolished General hospital which was known as the Sister Dora hospital), the view in the 1860s would have shown a mass of industrial activity. Scores of smoking, belching chimneys filled the background, with the railway running alongside the then polluted Fordbrook by the greenery of Walsall racecourse. To the railway, from the hospital, was a sloping grassy bank. It was on this bank that Sister Dora asked the local hospital committee to lay out a small pleasure garden, with flowers and shrubs to enable the patients to relax in fine weather. This request was duly granted and during summer days Sister Dora would be seen in attendance. Passenger and goods trains passed by every few minutes, each giving a special whistle to Sister Dora, who knew each driver by his whistle. She and her patients would wave until the train was out of sight.

One night in April 1872, a young railway fireman named William Chell was run over by a locomotive and he was carried into the Cottage hospital with one leg severely crushed. William's leg had to be amputated and it was seventeen weeks before he could leave the hospital. Through these long weeks of pain and shock, Sister Dora attended. She broke the rigid rule on visiting hours with a concession to all William's railway friends to visit him at any hour suitable to them. Owing to the unsociable hours that applied to maintaining railway schedules, this caused inconvenience to Sister Dora's hospital routine, but such was her bond with the railwaymen that nothing was too much trouble.

On 15 October 1875, the worst accident in Walsall's history occurred at the works of the Walsall Iron Co. in Green Lane, Birchills. A tuyere supporting the blast furnace collapsed, cascading molten metal over a number of workers standing nearby. The Cottage hospital had to be almost emptied of patients to accommodate the serious burns cases. This was Sister Dora's finest hour as she nursed the victims for weeks, mostly in vain, working to the point of exhaustion. Treatment of burns was primitive at this time, and subsequently infection prevailed, and the Cottage hospital had to close. A temporary hospital was authorised, with premises being found in a large, three-storey house in Bridgeman Place, which belonged to the L&NWR. This house was infested with rats and was in a most unsatisfactory position. It was situated only a few yards from the tracks on the 'up' side of Walsall station, where flooding from the Bridgeman Street subway left obnoxious smells, and the constant noise from passing trains gave no respite to seriously ill patients. Sister Dora visited the station and requested the engine drivers and firemen not to whistle or loose off steam when passing through. The word evidently passed along the railway system for Sister Dora was quoted as saying. 'You would never believe how quiet it is now in Walsall station'.

15

From Bustling Steam Shed to Wildlife Haven – the Creation of Mill Lane Nature Reserve

After the closure of Ryecroft shed in 1965 until its demolition in 1970, the land lay fallow for a number of years, until finally in 1988 it was sold to Walsall Metropolitan Borough Council to be used as public open space.

In 1991, the area of 8.72ha (22 acres) was landscaped thanks to a derelict land reclamation scheme, resulting in the creation of footpaths and wildlife habitats such as woodland, grassland and lakes.

To help with this transformation from wasteland to wildlife haven, in 1992 Walsall Countryside Services of Walsall MBC helped to produce a management plan detailing proposals to conserve and enhance the wildlife, access and recreational value of the site. Since 1996, under the management of Walsall Countryside Services, the wildlife habitats have thrived, creating a diverse mix of wetland, grassland, woodland, marsh, heath and open water, enjoyed by many visitors for walking, fishing and the appreciation of nature. Due to the value of the wide variety of wildlife the site holds, in 2001 it was designated as a Site of Importance for Nature Conservation (SINC), to help protect its important wildlife habitats.

Despite all this attention, however, and the years of local people's enjoyment of the site, it was realised that it had never been officially named! Therefore, in early 2002 a public competition was launched to find a name for the nature reserve, from choices relevant to the various periods of the site's history. When the results were collated it was found that 'Mill Lane Nature Reserve' was by far the most popular choice.

In order to realise Mill Lane Nature Reserve's full potential as a place for local people to enjoy wildlife and nature, a project was developed to create a way-marked nature trail, full colour on-site information boards and a site leaflet, in partnership with Walsall Deaf People's Centre. After working with the local community – collecting their memories, anecdotes and views – the project was completed in 2003, and was funded by 'The Local Heritage Initiative', which is a national grant scheme that helps local groups to investigate, explain and care for their local landscape. The initiative is a partnership between the Heritage Lottery Fund, Nationwide Building Society and the Countryside Agency.

The shed before demolition had made much impact, this time seen from the Mill Lane side of the shed. (R. Selvey)

The shed fully demolished on 15 August 1970. In this view looking to the 'Alps', note the air-raid shelter on the hill top in the centre. (R. Selvey)

Looking from above and behind the shed (the 'Alps') towards Ryecroft Junction after demolition. (R. Selvey)

Class 25 diesel 7609 running light past the shed site on the Cannock line, 20 June 1970. (R. Selvey)

Front cover of the full-colour leaflet printed to promote the Mill Lane nature reserve that now occupies the site of Ryecroft engine shed.

The shed site today looking towards the 'Alps'. Its role as a local nature reserve is very much in evidence. (Jack Haddock Collection)

During the historical research sessions as part of the project, it was found that the nature reserve's history was amazingly rich and varied, dating back to the eleventh century AD and included a corn mill, mining, railways and a dog pound! The history is summarised within the Mill Lane Nature Trail leaflet, available free from Walsall Countryside Services.

Since then, the amazing history and valuable nature conservation habitats of the reserve have continued to be enjoyed by many visitors, managed by Walsall Countryside Services for the benefit of future generations of local people and wildlife. For more information contact Walsall Countryside Services on 01922 459813.